RESEARCH TIME HOW INFLUENCES CONSUMER BEHAVIOR

JOHN LOK

Contents

Preface

Introduction

Consumer behavioral research topic is general businessmen whom have interest to investigate. They aims may expect to find whether how and why the consumers select to buy the product or research whether which factots can influence consumers' choices to change their consumption attitudes or desires to select to buy the product or consume the service.

In this book, however, I aim to research whether time factor can influence the consumer individual consumption desire to be changed either to choose to buy this product or consume this service or choose to buy another product or consume another service to replace the consumer whose original preference choice. If time factor can influence any one consumer individual consumption choice to be changed easily.

I research this topic aim to let any product sellers, service providers, consumers can understand that whether it is possible that time factor can influence consumer behaviors to be changed easily in order to let product sellers or service providers may attempt prediction when their consumer behaviours may be influenced to change by time variable influence or their consumer behaviors may be influenced to change in what consumption environments or situations. Also, I shall give opinions to attempt to explain whether what advantages can attract to persuade the consumer whom changes consumption desire from time variable factor influence suddenly.

All of above questions, I shall indicate sample cases to let readers to understand clearly. The topic is suitable to students to research aim, or businessmen whom aim to attempt to make predictions when their consumer behaviors will be influenced to change by time variable factor.

Prologue

CHAPTER ONE

Consumer behavioral factors influence theory

To research consumer behavior, it has different theory to explain why and how the consumer is influenced to make the choice by different factors. For example, utility theory,it explains that consumers make choices based on the expected outcomes of their decisions. They are viewed as rational decision makers and they only consider self interest.

Utility theory views consumer is as a " rational economic man". However, the factors influence consumer behaviors may include these activities, such as need recognition, information search, evaluation of alternatives, the building of purchase intention , the act of purchasing choice, consumption and finally disposal. Hence, it seems that all the consumer's activities in whose purchase processes. They will influence their choice. For example, when the property purchase consumer , he plans to research different kinds of properties information concern price, location, housing areas, room numbers, building facilities and environment facilities. He will find some sample target properties information to make comparison in order to decide to buy which of property is the most suitable to satisfy his living need.

However, it is not only one activity for the property purchase buyer in his decision making process. It also include evaluation of alternatives activitiy when he ensures the accurate property information number in order to evaluate whether which one of all these property choices is the most suitable one. Hence, it explains that property information research and evaluation of alternatives both activities are needed to spend much time for this property buyer. If he does not plan to find one property to live in short time, it is possible that he can spedn one month, even more than one month or more than three months time to do the only property information gathering activity.

Hence, it seems that time factor is not the main factor to influence the property buyer to do property purchase decision immediately. Otherwise, if the property buyer plans to find one new property to live within one month. Then, time factor is possible one important factor to influence this property purchase chocie decision. For example, if he felt that he needs more time to spend to gather information concerns the large house area size and the properties have more than three bathrooms and/or bedrooms properties information. Then, he will be possible not to find any this kinds of all property information. So, it means that all these properties won't be his choice. It is because long time property information gathering activity factor influnce.

I assume that the property buyer is a economic man and he does not spend much time to do the property information gathering activity. So, this kind of property needs him to spend long time to gather properties inforation in order to make this kind of properties comparison. Moreover, because he expects to live one new property within one month. So, he only chooses the properties, they have less than three bedrooms and/or bathrooms to gather sample properties information in order to make property purchase decision within one month. Hence, the time variable factor can only influence the property purchaser when he/she needs to make decision to buy one new property to live in the short time. If some kinds of properties choices number has a lot and the property buyer feels to let that he/she must need to spend long time to find the suitable properties number to make evaluation alternatives comparison behavior.

Then, the time variable limiting pressure factor will be possible the main factor to influence the property buyer's choice in order to make the most suitable kind of property purchase decision. Hence, it is one case example of how time limiting pressure factor can influence consumer purchase choice decision, such as property purchases market case. The reason explains why the property buyer needs to spend time to do property information gathering. I assume that general property buyer behave rationally in the economic sense. They won't only believe property agent individual property photos advertisement , it concerns where the property location is and facility etc. information on property photos in order to evaluate whether the property price is reasonable to pay. Generally, property buyers need to attempt to gather property information and visit the different actual property locations to make choice. So, general property consumers would have to be aware of all the available different kinds of properties consumptin options from themselves properties information gathering and the properties agents' verbal properties introduction both be capable of correctly rating each property alternative and the available to select the optimum course of the final property purchase action.

Hence, in the property purchase and sold market, limiting time pressure factor will be important influential factor to decide whether the kinds of properties will be option to some property buyers when they feel need to find one suitable property to buy in short time. Otherwise, in some food consumption market , time limiting pressure factor will not be the main factor to influence consumer option. Such utility theory indicates consumers are as one rational economic man, whom do not expect to spend much time to do any options evaluation decision making.

However, in coffee market, buying a coffee comes almost automatically and does not need much information search. Hence, time limiting pressure factor won't one main factor to influence coff consumer to choose to buy the kind of coffee to drink. However, there are other factors to influence coffee consumers' kind of coffee drinking option from cultural, social, personal or psychological factors. So, coffee taste producer can follow these factors to estimate how coffee consumers might behave in the future when making any kinds of coffee making purchasing decisions.

Firstly, social factor can affect coff consumer behavior significantly. Every coffee consumer has someone around influencing his/her coffee buying decisions. The important social factors include reference groups, family, role and status , e.g. when the coffe buyer has high income job and his friends have good educational level and high income. Then, he will compare his reference group, such as his friends' coffee buying behavior choosing which kinds of coffee taste to drink in habits or lifestyles. If he chooses the kind of coffee taste to drink, its price is cheaper to compare his friends' drinking coffee tastes. Then, he may be influenced to follow his friends to drink the same kinds of coffee taste in order to keep their same social status and role between him and his friends.

Secondly, the coffee consumers will be influenced how to choose which kinds tastes of coffee to drink by personal factors, such as his age, life cycle state, occupation, economic situation , lifestyle and personality and self-concept. Age related factors are such as taste in food, e.g. the kinds of coffee taste. Although, coffee price is cheap, but if the coffee consumer's income is more and he/she can often spend to buy different kinds of taste coffees to drink. Then, his/her income level will have much purchasing power to influence his/her purchasing behavior. Hence the coffee consumer's frequency of consumption of different kinds of coffee taste drinking choice behavior will represent whether his/her income level is high or low in possible. For example, the consumer needs to go to automatic coffee shop to buy at least three cups or more different kinds of high class good taste coffee brands to drink per week. Although, these high class coffee brands' prices are higher than the low class of coffee brands. But the coffee consumer still only buys any one of these kinds of high class brands' coffee taste to drink. Hence, it seems that this coffee consumers ought have high income to let hims to buy at least three cups of high class brand of coffee taste to drink from automativ coffee ship per week.

So, income factor can influence the coffee consumer to choose either coffer purchase from supermarket or coffee drinking at automatic coffee shop. If the coffee consumer only chooses to buy coffee from supermarket, due to the bottles of different kinds of brand coffee can provide more different tastes of coffees choices from shelves to let him to buy to drink at home. So, it seems that the coffee consumer's income level is low in general. Otherwise, if the coffee consumer only chooses to go to automtic coffee shop to buy the high class brands of coffee tastes to drink at least thre times or more per week. It may mean that the coffee consumer has high income level to support him/her to often go to automatic coffee shop to buy different kinds of high class coffee tastes to drink frequently every week. Som high or low income level factor can influence every coffee consumer individual drinking coffee behavioral options.

Moreover, when the coffee consumer is younger coffee consumer will be possible to buy much coffee to drink. Because younger age people can accept to drink coffee habitually more than older age people. Also, it is possible that younger peopler feel often drinking coffee behavior will help them to bring more health feeling and /or raising nervous to learn , due to they need often to go to schools to study. Otherwise, older age people feel often drinking coffee behaviors won't help them to bring more health and they do not need to raise nervous to learn.

Finally, even, cultural difference factor will influence coffee consumers number fo any countries. For example, western countries'people like to drink any kinds of coffee tastes traditionally. Asia countries' people like to drink any different kinds of teas tastes traditionally. So, different kinds of teas tastes will be asia people's traditional drinking substitute to replace different kinds of coffee tastes more easily. Hence, culture difference will be one factor to influence asia coffee buyers number. So, it seems that time limiting pressure factor won't influence coffee consumers' coffee taste choices to different kinds of high class or low class brands, visiting coff shops or visiting supermarkets choices, frequent or not frequent coffee drinking behaviors.

CHAPTER TWO

How and why time limiting pressure influences consumer choice

Can consumer buying decisions be influenced by time limiting pressure. For these three situations, they will influence consumer hoe makes different buying decision, e.g. in the little time available, but the consumer needs to do more effort needed to choose to buy which kind of product among variety kinds of product choice or in a moderate amount of time available, or a considerable amount of time available. In this first situation, the consumer can not real attempt to find any weaknesses or unique characteristics of the products, because it has no enough time to allow whom to choose. So, his/her product evaluation won't be th most accurate to satisfy his/her needs because little time can only allow him/her to find some weaknesses of the products. Otherwise, in the final situation, because the consumer has a considerable amout of time to allow him/her to attempt to find the weaknesses and/or strengths characteristics of the products choice. So, he/she ought do the more reasonable or accurate evaluation of these products to choose the most effective economic beneficial product to buy. Thus, it seems that time limiting pressure factor can influence the consumer to make more rational or more reasonable economic beneficial consumption decision making to buy the product or consume the service.

Thus, a consumer buying decision will require these situations to do buying decisions, they may include either little time and conscious effort or a moderate amount of time and effort or a considerable amount time and effort. The products may include cheap products/services , e.g. fruit, DVD, university courses, computers, facial services, surgeries, sport shoes, reference books, soft drinks, magazines as well as expensive products/ services, e.g. cars, houses, luxury goods, e.g. jewellery, female hand bags, holiday travelling entertainment. So, any expensive or cheap products or services, the consumer will need to spend either little or moderate or considerable amount time to do gathering information about the different kinds of products or services in order to find which brand of product or service can bring more economic benefit when he/she chooses to use the product or consume the service. He/she will compare his/her preference sample brands limiting number of products or services choices to decide to buy the brand of product or consume the brand service easily. However in the consumer's consuming decision making process, he/she will need to spend either little or moderate or a considerable amount of time to do the evaluation and choice consumption behavior. It means that time limiting pressure factor will influence the consumer how to make consumption choice consequently.

What are the impacts of reduced branding on consumer choice and time limiting pressure to influence consumer behavior? When one consumer needs to choose products to buy one in a time limiting pressure consumption environment, when branding on packaging is reduced, e.g. the brand of product has 10 different style of packages to let consumer choice, but it reduces to only 5 different style of packages to let consumer choice. How does it influence the consumer decision making when the consumer has little time to allow to choose these 5 different style of packages ? For example, when the consumer expects to spend only 10 minutes to choose any one style of package to buy drom this brand product. Currently, this brand of produxt has reduced different style of packages number from 10 to 5. Do you feel that the consumer will feel easy to do decision making to choose to buy the most attractive style of package product from this brand's 5 different style of packages choices? Is 10 minutes consumption choice time enough to let the consumer to make final purchase decision from these brand's 5 different style of packages choice? Will the time limiting pressure be reduced , due to this brand's 10 style packages are reduced to 5 style packages to let the consumer to choose within the 10 minutes expected limiting consumption choice time.

It is one interesting psychological consumption behavior to research whether the brand's reducing different style of packages number factor will influence the consumer to do the decision making in the short time in the time limiting pressure environment. For toothpaste, shapmo products example, if the brand of these products' style packages choice is reduced to 5 style packages from 10 style packages choice. When one consumer finds the brand of toothpaste or shampo has only 5 style packages on the shelves in supermarket. If the consumer has moderate or considerate amount time to let him/her to choose these both kinds product any one style of packages to buy. The 5 style packages to these both inds of products will be impossible to satisfy the consumer's choice need because he/she haas much time to stay in supermarket to choose. Otherwise, if the consumer has little time to allow to stay in the supermarket , e.g. ony 10 minutes. Then, he/she expects to spend only 10 minutes consumption choice time to do buying decision making within 10 minutes. These both kinds of the brand's products, its styl of packages choice number is reduced to 5, it is possible to satisfy the consumer's choice need to buy this brand of product either toothpaste or shampoo and both of thee brand of products to be chose to buy in the supermarket. So , the reducing style of package number to let consumer choice will be seem to let the conumer to do buying decision making in the limiting time pressure consumption environment.

In fact , package is such a visual to influence consumer decision making in the short time or personal limiting time choice process. If the product has more attractive package design, the it can bring more attention effort to influence the consumer to choose to buy the product in the short time information transfers to influence the consumer decision making to choose to buy more easily , when he/she is active in communication process. So, package, communicating with consumer in the selling place , has become an essential factor to influence the choice of consumer.

Scientific researches have proved that package decisions can attract consumer attention, transfer the desirable information abou tthe product, position , the product in consumer conscious, differentiate and identify of among similar kinds of products. In that way elements of package influence consumer decision making process and can determine the choice of consumer and the package itself can become more competitive advantage.

However it is not absolute that the brand of product has more package choices, it must have more customers to choose to buy its product. For example, there are two brands of shampoo in the supermarket shelf. One brand shampoo has 5 different style of packages and 5 different fruit productive elements to cause similar fresh fruit smells to attract consumers to buy. Another brand shampoo has 3 different style of packages and 3 different fresh fruit smells to attract consumers to buy in the same shelf location also. When one supermarket customer has little time to expect to stay in the supermarket, e.g. he expects only to stay the supermarket maximum to 15 minutes. he expects to buy one bottle shampoo and meats and fruits and vegatables within 15 minutes. Hence, he expects only to spend about 5 minutes to choose one brand of shampoo product as well as he demands to spend maximum 10 minutes to buy other foods within 15 minutes. When he stays in the shampr shelf location, he finds only two brands of shampoo products are displayed on the same shelf location. One brand of shampo has 5 different style packages to let him to choose, but he feels that these 5 diffeent style packages are not very attractive. Otherwise, the another brand of shampo has only 3 different style packages to let him to choose, but he feels that the 3 different style packages are very attractive. Due to he feels time causes pressure to choose these two brands of shampoo immediately. So, he does not want to spend more time more than 5 minutes to choose on brand of shampoo to buy. He will be influenced by the brand of different styles of packages more attraction to influence his buying decision making obviously. So, whether the shampoo brand's package is attractive or not, it will influence the consumer's buying decision making to choose either to buy the brand's shampo product in preference.

So, the more packages choice to the brand's product which may not mean that it has high opportunity to influence consumers' attention. Otherwise, the attractive package element if more important to compare right number of packages choices. Consumer package can influence these elements, e.g. colour, size, imageries, graphics, materials, smell, brand name, producer/ country, information, special offers. Of the brand of products can have much attractive elements. Then, it can attract consumers to choose to buy the brand's attractive package products in short time decision making process, such as perception of needs, search for information , evaluation of alternatives, decision making, behavior after purchase. Such as supermarket case, I assume that any supermarket consumers do not expect to spend much time to choose which brand of product is the most suitable or earning more economic benefit to buy when they need to stay the shelf to need spend much time to select which brand of product to buy in the supermarket. Because in general, supermarket consumers ought plan to buy more than one kind of product or food, even more usually. So, limiting time pressure factor will influence their decision making. Similarly, as my explanation indicates why although, the product had attractive package elements and its has many packages number choices, but it does not mean that it can win the similar product which has not more attractive packages, even it has more packages choices number to let supermarket consumers to choose. So, an attractive package element factor will have more influential and potential to cause supermarket consumers to choose to buy it in the supermarket limiting time pressure consumption environment.

CHAPTER THREE

How the time consumption pressure factor influences irrational consumption decision making

When one consumer has a large number of options, he/she will feel time pressure to cause whose accurate and reasonable evaluation. Then, the personal time limiting pressure factor will bring these questions: How does the time limiting pressure influence the consumer evaluation? Will the consumer personal limiting time pressure bring advantages and / or disadvantages in whom consumption decision making? How to help the consumer to solve short time decision problem when he/she encounters extreme time pressure an dchoice overload?

I shall assume every consumer is general one economic man. He/she feels time is important, he /she does not want to spend much time to choose one brand of product to buy among a number of brands of products choices. I also assume that any consumers decision making satisfaction, which is based on search until they found a sufficiently good item, or run not of time. So, it seems that which the consumer needs to buy one kind of product, but the product has a lot number of different brands to let the consumer to choose. The consumer ought need to spend much time to make choice decision making. However, consumer is one economic man, he/she ought not to search all different brands to decide whether which brand of product can bring the much economic value or utility value to choose to buy. So, in general, consumers will only choose sample brands of products to decide to buy the satisfied brand of product. For example, when the consumer needs to buy one television. The television has 20 brands of similar televisions to let he to choose. He will not spend much time to search these similar 20 televisions information. He will only gather sample 10 to 15 or less different brands of televisions to compare what their strengths and weaknesses, unique characteristics. Then, he will make decision to choose to buy the best television from these sample televisions. Hence, in general, consumers will feel time pressure when they feel need to spend much time to choose a lot different brands of similar products. Because they feel time is not enough to let they can do other important matters when they need to spend much time to do search information behavior when they need to buy any products ususally. Hence, it is general consumers psychology that they will feel real choice under time pressure and choice overload, when they have too much a lot of similar brands of products to let them have opportunity to choose to make decision making to buy only one brand of product.

However, when a brand of product is familiar and given its simplicity and familiarity to general consumers' acknowledgement. It will have perference advantage to attract or influence consumers' attention or consideration. So, when the market has similar different brands of products are available to let consumers to choose. The largest choice set is not large enough to create overload to influence the brand's sale when consumers need to spend much time to choose these different brands similar products to buy. Because when the brand's any products are familiar and given its simplicity and familiarity to general consumers' knowledgement. Then, it can build utility confidence to influence general consumers , it will be preference sample brand of product to do buying making option. Hence, the brand's familiarity factor will influence general consumers' preference buying decision making option. So, any product manufacturers need to concern how to build its brand familiarity to let many consumers to acknowledge in order to raise its competitive effort. Raising brand's familiarity may be a good method to solve consumer individual choice under time pressure overload , because when the brand of product is preference sample brand to any consumers. It's sale opportunity will also be raised. So, it brings the question: How can the brand of products can cause general consumers' preference choice. For food example, food brands were more likely to choose the implicitly preferred brand over the explicitly preferred one when choices were made under time pressure.

Imagining one customer enters a supermarket 10 minutes before closing time. He failed to write up a shopping list. So, when the staff is preparing to close store at the night, the consumer hurry trys not to for set too many of the ingredients for dinner . What brands of products , he opts for, as he can choose from a variety of similar foods, but time is short and the staff is looking at the consumer impatienty? It is possible that the consumer will probably quickly decide in favor of the foods he likes best, pay, and leave the evening.

Hence, supermarket consumer's first time feeling to the brand of food will influence whom choice. One target category and one attribute category share same response key: Pleasant vs unpleasant feeing, if the supermarket consumer has pleasant feeling when he sees the food photos and touchs the package of the brand of food to feel pleasant in the short supermarket closing time. Then, his pleasant feeling will be chooses to buy the brand of food to eat. Thus, the consumer individual pleasant or unpleasant feeling factor will influence whom consumption choice, such as this supermarket closing time pressure consumption.

In fact, many factors may influence whether consumer behavior is under more or less control. Hunger may influence control in the domain of eating behavior . So, such as the supermarket will close soon,it has store closing time pressure to influence the consumer needs hurry to make choice decision to buy food. If the consumer feels more hungry, he will not spend much time to find the right food to buy. He will be influenced by the different brand's food packages whether which brand of food package can bring a more pleasant to let him to feel, when he touchs and sees the brand of food package. He won't spend time to search whether the different kinds of brands of foods have how much different health elements because the supermarket will close store soon. So, he only depends his individual pleasant feeling to make final food purchase decision. If he feels all of the kinds of brands foods are unpleasant food packages when he sees and touchs them first time as well as he does not feel much hungry. Then, it is possible that he won't choose to any one food to eat. He will choose to go to restaurant to get dinner to replace buying food to cook to eat dinner at home at the night.

The another case is that time pressure concerns how on choice of information source impacts purchase decisions. When the consumer who buys one product , he needs to use the same number of information sources to search the product's information regardless of time pressure. Because he has more available time, he devotes more time , but only to selected the right sources to search information about the product. He will mostly use marketing dominant sources, e.g. magazine. he feels magazine can give more accurate information concerns to the product's good or bad quality real more reasonable and fair evaluation to let the consumer to acknowledge. so, when the consumer has much time to choose to buy which brand of product is the most best choice. He will buy magazine to find information. He believes magazine has more fair evaluation to different brands of product. It won't mislead consumers to make wrong decision making. Hence, in general, when consumers have much time to find information source to search which brand of product is more value to buy. They will attempt to buy consumer magazine to acknowledge whether the different brands of product , which have unique characteristics, strengths or weaknesses in order to compare them to make more accurate evaluation to choose to buy which brand of the kind product. When they have no time pressure to influence their choice process time to be shortened or reduced. Otherwise, these consumers will depend on newspapers, television, radio advertisments information sources when they feel time pressure controls their consumption choice decision making process time to be shortened or reduced. Hence, time pressure will be possible to influence consumer individual information source channel choice.

CHAPTER FOUR

Time pressure consumption decision making process characteristics

How we can predict or know the consumer time pressure in whom decision making process? Will it bring advantages or disadvantages to influence the businessmens' benefits? I shall indicate some different consumption situations or environments to explain what will be impacted to sale number is increased or decreased to businesses when the consumer feel time pressure to avoid whom behavioral consumption to the product or the service.

Firstly, I shall explain that what effects of product popularity and time pressure on online shopping behaviors are . Electronic ecommerce is popular to any countries, in special, US, UK, China large areas countries, because when one customer feels need to spend one hour even more time to catch any transportation tool to arrive the shop to buy the kind of product. Then, due to far distance reason, he/she will choose to apply internet to buy the kind of product . If the seller has website to let the consumers to choose online shopping. However, it seems that online shopping behavior can reduce the consumer individual time pressure, when he/she feels need to catch any kinds of transportation tool to arrive the shop to buy the product. Moreover, when the consumer can turn on home computer to enter its website to choose the styles of the kind of products, which one is the most situable to choose. He/she can spend time to search the different styles kinds of product information to compare and evaluate which brand of product will b whose purchase choice easily at home.

Hence, in psychological view, he/she can feel that spending time to search information from internet behavior which is more valuable and it can bring more economic benefit to make final purchase decision more than the behavior of spending long time to catch any transportation tools to visit the shop. Moreover, it is possible to bring failure risk that he/she wastes time to catch any transportation tools to visit the shop if he/she can not find any one of suitable product(s) to choose to buy. Hence, it seems the online shopping can influence the consumer reduced time pressure and wastes time to do any shopping decision.

This is online shopping's attractive strengths to the consumers when they need to spend long time to catch any kinds of transportation tools to visit the shop or when the consumer feels hurry to do other important matters, he/she can not allow himself/herself to spend long time to do his/her visiting the shop behavior. Moreover, another online shopping's advantage is that product popularity can be perceived by examining the information presended on websites. For example, research on onlin reviews confirms the review quantity presented with products become positively influences to consumers' purchase intention and it can persuade the online visitor can make decision to buy the product when he/she has enter the seller's online website to find the most suitable product to choose to buy more easily. Hence, it seems that it is more easy to persuade the online visitor to make final purchase decision more than visiting the shop , when the online visitor can attempt to do the click mouse behavior to enter the seller's online shop, such as website. Then, he/she will be influenced to view the seller's different kinds of colourful and attractive product pictures from the seller's wesite.

Consequently, it has much opportunity to persuade the consumer to do the final purchase decision. if the seller's website is attractive to persuade him/her to visit its website to find any new products more than five times, even tem times or every weak several times , even day one time frequently visiting behavior from internet channel. Hence, due to internet is convenient tool to let consumers to find any product informatons from the seller's website at home or public library , computer, or mobile phone. Consumers must find any product informations any time in any places easily. So, online shopping can reduce any consumers' time pressure to visit any shops to expect to achieve final consumption decision aim in possible. Thus, it seems that online shopping method can influence consumers to feel time saving and time presure reducing consumption both advantages more than visiting shops' shopping method when the consumer is living far away from the shop. When the consumer feels that he/she is experiencing situational time pressure, then, he/she will respond well to seek another time saving situational consumption environment. So , it explains when one consumer feels he/she has no much time to catch long time transportation tool to visit the shop on the day. When he/she has computer at home, he/she will attempt to type the shop name to research whether it has online shopping platform service from internet. Because he/she does not want to spend one hour, even more time to catch transportation tool to arrive the shop, when he/she can't walk to the shop in short time. Even, he/she may feel online shopping behavior won't influence his/her eating , sleeping, or recreational time to be reduced at home or any places , when he/she can behave the online shopping behavior at home or any where conveniently.

Consequently, promoting online shopping is as a time-saver is likely to be effective for these experiencing situational time pressure. Those with situational pressure would almost certainly welcome anything that would reduce their activity level and the demands on their time. In fact, there is really no adult learning method for store shopping because it is something everyone learns to do from early childhood. But for many adult consumers, they feel have interest to learn how to use internet and web to shopping. Some adult will feel interest and it is value to learn how to use internet channel to anticipate the complexity of shopping online. For example, Super Walmart cheap frocery store that carries many thousands of products and brands to let online shoppers won't feel confused when viewing its online merchant's home page with only a few menu items and links from its website. So, Super Walmart website can let online shoppers to feel difficult that they can save much time to enter any merchants' home page . They only need to view the Super Walmart's website ,then they can find any preference cheap grocercies to compare and evaluate which one(s) is (are) value to buy. So, Super Walmart's website can let global cheap grocery online shoppers feel it can help them to save time to find any merchant's products from internet conveniently. Consequently, online shopping will be one popular time saving consumption channel to reduce time pressure to some consumers nowadays.

Secondly, I shall explain that what determines purchase decisions for airline tickets when the traveller fees time stress. When a travelling planner has no enough time to prepare whose travelling journey, whether the time stress will influence he/she feels decision difficulties and frustration, when it will cause he/she needs to gather significant amounts of information to lead to make to choose which airline ticket is the most right choice? How and number of airline options and time pressure influence the airline ticket buyer's purchase decision?

However, there are both kinds of time pressures to influence the airline ticket buyer's airline choice decision, they focus on either real decision deadlines (physical time), such as the journey beginning day is any day of this week or tomorrow or subjective feeling of pressure with time (sense of urgency or psychological time), such as the traveller expects that he/she fears all airlines' all seats are full booked in this month. Moreover, he/she can plan to catch air plane to travel next month. So, he/she will attempt to gather any airlines' tickets prices, flight day and time and destination arrival and weather information in this month to avoid that it is too late to delay his/her next month travelling plan.

Hence, it seems that the effect of number of airlines choices and air tickets purchase deadlines (physical time limit) will influence how the traveller or air ticket buyer's purchase decision using secondary data to search of airline ticket. for example, if the traveller felt time is no enough to let him/her to go to travel agent to enquire any airlines' air tickets prices and seats and date and time air plan departure available time to concern the traveller's destination choice. Then, he/she will be probable to choose to buy electronic-ticket (e-ticket) from internet. If he/she has computer to link internet to gather any airlines' flying date and time and seat available information at home easily. Hence, it seems that one time pressure traveller will be probable to choose e-ticket purchase at home in preference. If the airline can provide online e-ticket purchase option to the time pressure traveller. Due to the pressure time traveller feels closer to departure, the negative impact of number of airline options is not as strong when he/she can view the airline's website to find the flight date, time and seat available information to purchase e-ticket to prebook the date and time to departure the traveller's country and to arrive his/her travelling destination information from the airline's website channel at home or anywhere any time conveniently. Hence, travel agency can bring a positive relationship between airline number of options and pre-booking airline that immediate possibility. When the time pressure traveller hopes the airline can build the good interactive relationship between number of options and decision time limit (number of days till planned travel effort on e-ticket purchase probabilities. So, if the airline website can let the traveller to predict when date and time is accurate available to arrive whom frequently destination choice country as well as the e-ticket's real price , it is not e-ticket preductive price and the real seats number available, it is not the estimated seats number available on the departure time and date to the travelling or arrival country destination. Then, all of these online information to the airline, which will raise the e-ticket pre-booking purchase chance to let the e-ticket buyer to make whose final e-ticket purchase choice decisin to win its e-ticket competitors easily.

Consequently, a real time e-ticket information can attract any time pressure e-ticket buyers to choose to buy its e-ticket (electronic airline ticket) more than visiting travel agent's paper airline ticket option when the travel feels hurry to buy airline ticket to travel in short time.

CHAPTER FIVE

Reducing time pressure consumption methods

How can sellers persuade consumers to choose to buy their products or consume their services in time pressure environment easily? It is a valuble research topic to concern how to know how consumer individual decision making to spend his/her available resources (time, money and efforts, or consumption relatd aspects) as well as how any why he/she chooses the preference brand to buy its any kind of products or consume its services, when he/she chooses to buy the brand of products or consume its services? Hence, marketers need to obtain an indepth knowledge of consumer buying behavior.

In any buying process, time factor will have about 10 % to 40 % to influence consumer decision. When the consumer feels hurry to consume, e.g. planning to go to travel, when he/she needs to choose to buy which airline's air ticket and what day and time is the right air ticket prebooking purchase decision right time choice; or enrolling which school to be choosed course to study decison, e.g. how long time is needed to be choose which school is the most suitable to provide the most suitable courses studying choce change; purchase warm clothes to wear in winter, when is the suitable time to choose to buy the cheaper warm clothers to prepare to wear in winter, e.g. Jan to Mar., April to June, July to Aug. month; when is the most suitable time to buy another new house to live, when the property consumer(buyer) has lived present house for long time, e.g. three years or more. All of these issues will include time factor to influence the consumer feels when he/she ought choose to buy the kind of product or consume the kind of service. However, the other factors will also include to influence his/her decision, e.g. family, friend relationship factor, advertising factor, social status factor, cultural difference factor, personal psychological need level or satisfactory level factor, young or old age factor, income level factor, economic environment factor, material enjoyable need factor etc. factors.

However, time pressure factor will be the consumer individual intrinsic (internal) psychological feeling factor, and it is the consumer individual intrinsic feeling to judge whether when he/she ought spend some money to buy the kind ofcnew product or the kind of consume service (what time is the most reasonable or the most suitable time) to make purchase choice decision. However, when the consumer feels hurry to make purchase decision. So, he/she will not hope to spend more time to gather more information to compare and evaluate which one is the right brand of product tochoose to buy or the right service to consume among different brands of products or services. Otherwise, if the consumer has more time or he/she can make the decision to buy any brand of product. Then, he/she ought spend more time to gather more information to compare and evaluate which one is the most suitable product choice to buy or which one is the right service choice to consume. So, time pressure factor will have some influence to any consumers to make decision about what time is the suitable time to buy the kind of product or consume the service. For example, heater product is usually when winter weather time, the heater products need number ought increase in winter weather time or season. But, it is possible that the heater products need number won't increase in winter season / weather possible, when one country , there are many householders or families , they have one heater number at least at home. Then, it is possible that these householders or families won't have consumption desires to buy one more heater product to use in winter at home, because they have had one heater to use at home in winter. So , when the country has have many customers number, they are using the kind of heater products at homes. Most people own at least one heater number factor will have possible to influence enough time available to cause they do not feel hurry to buy any heaters to use at homes, so, their do not feel time pressure to buy any heaters in short time. Because they do not plan to buy the kind of product to use at home in short time when they have one heater product at least to use at homes in present.

Hence, it brings this question: How to attract or persuade the customers, they are using the kind of product to let they feel time pressure to make decision to buy another new or same brand of product to replace to use? The product's better quality , long durable time useful, brand loyalty and past good purchase experience factors will influence him/her to feel time pressure to need to buy another new product in short time. So,when the consumer feel time pressure to make decision to purchase, he/she will choose when is the most right time to gather information, search, select, use and dispose of another new product to replace the old product in the short time.

Hence, the brand of product needs have good product motives, may be raised to the consumer's impluse, desires, considerations which make the buyer purchase the brand's new product to replace the present using product in order to achieve whose satisfactory needs to emotional product motives and rational product motives both. Moreover, persuading or encouraging the consumer feels he/she has real need to buy the kind of new product or replace the present old product (s), the brand of product marketer needs let the consumer feels these any one of nature of motive to raise his/her purchase decision desire in time pressure environment. The natures of motive may include: When the consumer feels desire for saving money, he/she will choose to buy it when the brand of product falls down, when he/she feels fear to be sickness, retirement, he/she will choose to buy insurance policy, when he/she feels pride, or high social status knowledgement, he/she will buy premium product , e.g. gold, expensive watch, car , when he/she feels fashion need, he/she will move house to live from rural to urban, or rural people imitate urban to learn to do their fashion living behavior, when he/she feels possession need, he/she will feel need to buy antiques for its future unique worth satisfactory feeling in possible, when he/she feels health need, he/she will choose to buy health foods, join memebership in health clubs, when he/she needs to enjoy comfortable feeling, he/she will feel need to buy micro-oven, washing machine to use at home, when he/she feels love and affection need, he/she will buy gift items to give to whose friends or families for presents in their birthday or lover day etc. special days to let they to feel happy. So, when the marketer can touch the consumer individual different nature of motives to satisfy his/her personal purchase feeling need and it can know how to influence them to feel that they have these any one of purchase motive needs in short time. Then, they will be persuaded to raise time pressure to make purchase decison to buy any kind of products in short time.

However, instead of attractive good product quality method can attempt consumers to make time pressure consumption behavior. The another method is brand loyalty building method, which can be attempted to encourage or persuade consumers to feel consumption desire need to make decision to buy the brand of any products in time pressure consumption environment. For example, when the consumers feel the brand is loyalty and it can build good image to his/her feeling , and this time pressure factor can inlfuence this brand of any products which has high discount price to attract the consumer individual attention , e.g. familiar brand high class cars, the good confident house agent's high class houses, and the expensive and infrequently buying items, come under this category. When their prices are fallen down to sell cheaper , e.g. twenty per cent discount or more than twenty percent discount sale price than the other similar competitive brands' any products' normal prices. Then, it is possible to let these expensive items' consumers have high involvement and high feeling need in time pressure consumption environment. Because they assume that this discount sale price will be short time sale price, e.g. after three months or next month etc. short time discount sale price in short time period. Then, these expensive items' prices will be raised to the normal sale price, even higher price. so, they have time pressure feeling to feel that it is right time to make consumption decision in order to avoid to lose these low price purchase benefit in this unpredictive cheap discount price purchase items. so, if the expensive item marketer can build long time good brand loyalty relationship to consumers. Then, it will have much influential effort to persuade consumers feel consumption desires need by its any extensive items in the unpredictive short term discount period, due to they do not want to loss this large discount purchase price chance. So, short time discounted sale price, it is another method to persuade consumers to choose to buy the brand's any products in short time pressure consumption environment.

The another persuading time pressure consumption method is that it can let consumers to think more habitual buying the kind of products. products like stationery, groceries, food etc. fall under this category. For example, when the consumer fees the brand of any products ,he/she has habitual purchase experience, of he/she feels that the brand's any products won't sell in market temporary, even he/she can not buy it to use again. Then, it is possible to infuence him/her to feel immediate purchase need to buy a lot of product or food number to keep to use or eat later in the time pressure environment, e.g. the food consumer buys the brand of any breads to eat in supermarkets habitually, but in this moth, he/she watchs TV advertisement to be acknowledge this brand of any breads won't be bought from any supermarkets as soon as possible. Hence, it is possible to influence him/her to plan to make choice to buy a lot of number of this brand of any breads in order to keep the enough of this brand of breads number to eat later. So, this brand of any breads sale loss in supermarkets that will cause the habitual food consumers of this brand of breads, whom make consumption choice to buy a lot number of this brands any breads in short time suddenly. Because they are eating this brand of any kinds of breads habitually. They feel much eating need to lot number of this brand of any breads in short period, because it can satisfy their habitual taste needs of this brand's any kinds of breads. So, brand loyalty and habitual consumption to the kind of product or food , ehich will result simply from the habit and it can influence the consumers feel consumption need to buy the brand's any kinds of products or foods when they feel that they may not buy it again or they can not earn discount advantage after the short time. So, any one of these sale strategies will have possible to raise the consumer individual consumption desire to the brand of products in the short time pressure consumption environment. Also it needs to spend much time to gather information in order to make purchase decision, because the brand had built confidence to consumers when they feel this brand's any products or foods are better to compare the similar brands' any products or foods habitually. So, time pressure consumption environment will persuade them to feel consumption desire to buy this brand's any products or foods in short time. When, they fer that they can not buy any more for this brand's any kinds of products or foods or discounting price in this final short purchase time.

In conclusion, these factors can influence consumer behaviors to be changed to feel time pressure need to do purchase decision making behavior from encough time gathering information available feeling behavior. They have these same views, e.g. habits and routines are very influential, particularly for behaviors repeated daily in a semi-automatic fashion. The consumer's past purchas experience to the brand's products, positive or negative emotion to the brand's products, and the brand's familization, recognition are strong influence , the information available , it is the consumer's mind and the relative important information given to let the consumer knows form different advertisement medias matters for decision making, greating between pieces of information and can be influenced by personal psychological timing limited pressure, the consumer's comparison to differences in price or other characteristics, many pursue value (or in bargain), and compare to alternatives or past knowledge, consumer personal greater value on the immediate future and heavily disocunt future costs or savings to the brand of product, feeling simple and easy decision making process to the product , it can lead the consumer to avoid to spend long time to make purchasing decision and the consumer will easy to choose to buy the product when he/she feels have a loss value if he/she does not decide to buy the product in the short time. SO, it seems that when the marketer can motivate the consumer's consumption desire to feel saving money, promote health, avoid waste time and less nervous workload to gather information for comparison and evaluation alternatives aim. It is seen favorably by the consumer personal time pressure purchase decision making and sense of justice influence factors.

However, sociologists have categorised the motives for consumption behaviors in the short time by the fundamental consumption decision making needs or wants which they satisfy, e.g. having a clear understanding what benefits, characteristics, economic value to the brand's any products , feeling consumption decision making process is a leisure activity. These drivers for consumption behaviorw will either bring positive or negative to influence the consumer personal emotion, either owning enough time available or time pressure environmental impacts can be seen to influence whether the consumer feels he/she needs how long time to be spent to make comparison and evaluate alternatives in order to make final purchase choice in whom decision making process. Hence, the consumer himself/ herself time pressure consumption decision making feeling, it can bring positive purchase choice influence,when the marketer can build brand loyalty to let many consumers to feel in the market. Otherwise, if the marketer can not build brand loyalty to let many consumers to feel, but consumers feel time pressure to compare and evaluate its any products to other similar brands of products in the competitive market. Then, its products may be not the preference choices the many customers among the different brands of products choices. So, building long time brand loyalty relationship to satisfy consumers' needs, it will bring positive preference purchase choice to raise the sale effort to the brand of any products when consumers need to make purchase choice in time pressure consumption environment, e.g. seasonal discount sale period, products or foods shortage supply period, without any forever sale possibility in market. Hence , it seems that brand loyalty building factor will influence any brands of products /foods /service sale or provison number to be raised or reduced in possible. Also, it can explain why and how it has close cause and effect relationship between time pressure consumption environment and the brand loyalty building to the brand of products/foods/services to any marketers nowadays.

CHAPTER SIX

What are the in-store and out-store factors influence supermarket fast moving consumer decision

It is one interesting question: How can the brand of product seller influence the supermarket/store fast-moving consumers' more visual attention when the supermarket/store visitor is hurry to make decision to choose to buy which brand of product in time pressure environment? Supermarket/store fast-moving consumers do not usually spend much time to say in any supermarket shelf locations to choose numerous similar alternative brands of products. However, I assume the fast-moving supermarket/store consumer's decision is dependent on the interaction between the supermarket different shelf location sale environment and the mind of the consumer. So, the eye tracking explores this rapid processing that lacks conscious access or control to any supermarket or store consumers.

It brings this question: How product packing and placement (as in-store factors) and recognition, preferences, and choice task (as out-of-store factors) which will influence the supermarket / store consumer individual decision making process through visual attention. In split-second decision making, the ability to recognize and comprehend a brand of supermarket/ store product can significantly impact preferences. Hence, how the supermarket/store consumer's eye truly sees what whom mind is prepared to influence how much consumption desire to choose to buy the brand's product in short tim decision making process when he/she stays in the shelf location, it has less than ten or more than ten different kinds of brands products or foods to let the visitor to choose in the supermarket or store. Brand owners and product developers will feel responsibilities to overcome promotion or advertising or communicaton challenge in order to let consumers to know their products are launched on the market. However, it is not until the product reaches the supermarket shelf that has good quality to the effort is judged whether it has how much sale number every day in the supermarket. The judges are the consumers themselves how to make decision quickly through the personal time pressure environment with minor package information processing in the supermarket.

What does it take to be consider an option to influence the consumers' minds on visual attention in point-of-purchase decision making ? The supermarket's in-store activities and the consumer personal out-of-store activities will influence how his / her visual attention to the brand of products in the supermarket / store any shelf locations when he/she is walking to pass any shelf locations. So, it seems that any supermarkets or stores brands of products sale number , it has relation to every supermarket or store visitors' visual attention throughout the point to point (shelf to shelf) decision making process in the supermarkets / stores. So, how much does the supermarket's visitors' time spending to obtain attention to the brand of produc? it will have possible to influence the brand of any products' sale number in the supermarket/store. Hence, in this limited timeframe, the consumer enters a decision making process that is in itself influenced by in-store and out-of-store both factors.

I shall explain what is supermarket / store space quality factor, e.g. top level versus floor level to different shelf variable height, weigh , or shelf space location factor as well as the product price elasticity and price-quality relationship to the brand of products both factors to influence every consumer decision making in supermarket/store. The in-store factor is more influential factor to compare out-of-store factor to influence consumers' decision in supermarket. For example, where the shampoo brand products are locating to be put on the shelf , it can influence the point to point behavior of shampoo product habitual buyers. If the buyer habitually chooses the shampoo brand products in the shelf location. Also, if all of the shampoo brand products are moved to another shelf locations to display its different kinds of shampoo products to cause the habitual buyer needs to spend much extra time to find where the another new shelf location is displaying the brand's shampoo products.

In this situation, information processing has a heightened decision making role as the buyer needs to spend much time to find where the brand's displayed shampoo products' shelf location to make non-habitual decision making between options. For habitual decisons, the consumer's visual attention is reduced to measuring visual search. However, when the brands of any shampoo products are moved to another new shelf location to display its different kinds of shampoo products. So, the act of another shelf new location search , it will influence the habitual shampoo buyer's visual attention to consider the brand of any shampoo products which are usually used to wash to his/her hair habitually. When he / she can find the other new brands of shampoo products are displayed on the old shelf displayed location of the brand of shampoo products. Hence, the traditional shelf displayed location to the brand of products, when the brand of products are moved to another new displayed shelf locations. This in-store factors that will influence traditional cosnumers through visual attention concerns to this brand of products more or less.

So, supermarket traditional shelf displayed variable location to the brand of products factor, which will have influence to the traditional consumers' visual attention to do either buying the brand's products or buying another brand's products to replace it, when the traditional consumer feels difficult that he/she needs to spend extra longer time to find whether where is the traditional useful product's displayed shelf location. Then, it will be possible to influence the traditional consumer's traditional purchase decision to the brand's product, and he/she will choose to buy another brand of product to replace when it can be displayed to the shelf location to attract the consumer's visual attention more.

It is one important in-store shelf displayed factor to influence the traditional fast-moving consumer individual purchase decision making behavioral change in any supermarkets or stores when they feel hurry to do personal time pressure consumption decision to make purchase final decision in the point to point counter purchase (the brand's of products are moved from the traditional shelf location visual attention moves to the strange shelf location visual attention) in supermarket time pressure consumption environment.

Hence, in supermarket time pressure consumption environment, in -store and out-of-sore both factors can influence fast-moving consumer individual purchase decision making. The in-store factors can influence product packaging, product placement components as well as the out-store factors can influence choice task, preference and brand recognition components. So, it is common to influence supermarket consumers choose do personal time pressure purchase consumption decision of visual attention purchase behaviors. The different brands' products are displayed to different shelf locations in order to cause shelf displaying products' different decision making effect.

However, instead of shelf displaying location factor, package will also influence consumers' decision making, due to the influence of minute differences in packaging design on visual attention. When, the supermarket consumer feels the brands are not familiar or unfamiliar. Then, he/she will spend more time to evaluate and verify the unfamiliar brands' products whether which one is value to buy in her/his decision making process. He/she will feel visual attention need in order to evaluate in set of brand alternatives to make conscious demand mind cognitive effort by involving working memory. So, if the product's package is attractive, even the consumer is unfamiliar the brand's any product choices which are displayed on the shelf location in the supermarket. The brand's attractive package factor can influence the consumer to raise whom visual attention. Then, the attractive package factor can increase much visual attention chance to many consumers when they are walking to pass through the unfamiliar brand's any products' shelf displaying location considerably. So, it explains when attractive package factor may solve the visual attention problem to fast-moving consumers when they are visiting one strange supermarket to find anywhere unfamiliar brand's products' shelf displaying locations. Because they are the non-traditional consumers to the unfamiliar brand's products, they won't be influenced to choose either buying or not buying the unfamiliar brand's products. When the unfamiliar brand's products are moved to another new shelf displayed location. So, if the unfamiliar brand has attractive package to let the non-traditional consumers feel visual attention when they are passing through the strange shelf displayed location. Then, it can raise purchase chance to the non-traditional consumers target number when they are staying in the strange supermarket. In conclusion, the brand of products' shelf displaying location and package factors may bring much influence to any traditonal or non-traditonal consumer behaviors in supermarket or store time pressure consumption environment.

CHAPTER SEVEN

What consumption is most influenced in preference choice by time pressure

What kinds of services or products are most influenced to consumer behavioral change by time pressure? Can time pressure factor influence more preference to other factors, such as age, culture, income level, habitual shopping, family or friend relationship etc. factors to influence consumer behavioral choice to these kinds of services or products in consumption market? I shall indicate some kinds of services or products consumption models to explain how time pressure can influence consumers to choose to consume its services or buy its products.

Firstly, for theme park entertainment industry example, has it time pressure to cause any theme park visitors, e.g. Walt Disney entertainment theme park to influence them to feel time pressure to enjoy their emotions to play any entertainment machine facilities and it brings negative emotion to choose the entertainment theme park entertainment consumption activities.

For Walt Disney entetainment theme park example, every visitor needs to pay a fixed ticket fee to enter Disney theme park. So, however, he/she chooses to play how many number of entertainment activities facilities, e.g. only one entertainment playing facility, or more than one entertainment playing facilities. The Disney visitor needs to pay the same ticket fee to enter Disney. So, it will cause th visitors feel unfair , they do not choose to play any entertainment facilities or play only less number of entertainment facilities. Because they need to pay the same ticket price to same to the visitors, who choose to play many entertainment facilities number in

Disney. So, it brings this question: Does the Disney visitor feel time pressure when he/she chooses to play many number of entertainment facilities , but he/she will not enjoy to carry on other activities in Disney, e.g. shopping, visiting cinema to watch movies, walking around the whole Disney anywhere to view scene activities. Because US Disney entertainment theme park is very large . It has not only entertainment facilities to attract visitors to play. It has many places are value to visitors to visit or enjoy the other free charge entertainment activities , such as visiting Disney gardens, visiting ocean park, visiting Disney cinema to watch free movies, view scene or seeing free charge ocean animal performance shows , going to Disney shopping centres to shopping, visiting Disney library to read books, visiting Disney ocean park to view different kinds of beautiful fishes non-entertainment machine facility playing activities. All of these activities are value to any Disney visitors to choose to play or visit, instead of entertainment machine facilities activities. So, if one visitor hopes only to spend one day in US Walt Disney entertainment theme park. He/she will feel hurry to choose to play any machine entertainment facilities, or he/she won't choose any machine entertainment facilities to play in Disney because he/she also hopes to play other non-machine entertainment facilities activities, e.g. visiting garden, visiting ocean park, visiting library, visiting cinema to watch free movies, visiting garden to play free charge boats water entertainment activities, watching ocean animal show performance etc. different kinds of entertainment activities, even walking around anywhere fun and excite places in Disney theme park. Hence, the Disney visitor will feel time pressure to choose either playing any kinds of entertainment machine facilities or visiting different places in the whole one day in Disney.

Hence, time pressure factor may influence any one of Disney visitors how to choose any entertainment activities to spedn time in Disney. It will bring this question: Because the Disney ticket price is fixed fee, can the Disney visitor will feel unfair to cause negative emotion, if the Disney visitor feels time pressure to choose to play any kinds of machine entertainment activities or doing other non-machine entertainment activities in the Disney visitor's limited timeframe, during he/she stays in Disney? So, it seems that time pressure psychological factor will may influence some Disney visitors to feel unhappy, negative emotion, when they feel their entertainment activities choices are wrong or doing wring entertainment decision making in his/her limited timeframe. Consequently, time pressure factor will influence some feeling time pressure Disney visitors won't choose to enter Disney again. Hence, time pressure factor can have much influence to theme park visitors' behavioral change, instead of whether the entertainment theme park's machine entertainment facilities are attractive or enjoyable playing or how many entertainment facilities are supplied to let visitors to play in the entertainment theme park. So, entertainment theme park service providerd need to consider whether their ticket prices are reasonable to let visitors feel, if they do not want to reduce theme park visitors number seriously.

The another example is restaurant food service industry. Can time pressure influence food consumers to choose the restaurant to eat? Instead of food taste, price, seats available providing, restaurant location, public transportation facilities available etc. factors, which can influence the food consumer individual choice to the restaurant.

Is time pressure another one main factor to influence food consumers choice to the restaurant? In what suitation, food consumers will feel time pressure to influence whose preference restaurant choice? I assume that the restaurant 's price is reasonable, public transportation facility is convenient to catch to go to the restaurant, food taste is acceptable to the food consumer. Although all above these factors are accepted to the food consumer . But when the food consumer feels hurry to hope to find one restaurant to eat and he/she hopes to spend less time to sit down to eat in the restaurant , e.g. less than one hour. Then, the food consumer will compare all the restaurants are near to whose working place or school , if he/she is one student or one working person. Because he/she needs to eat lunch to go to school or go to office to work. So, the restaurant's food taste, price is not the main factor to influence him/her to choose to eat. Otherwise, whether the restaurant needs him/her to spend how long queue time to wait, or/and the restaurant needs how long cooking time to let him/her to eat, the restaurant needs him/her to walk how long time to arrive the restaurant. All of these factors concern " efficient cooking time, queue waiting time serice performance" issues to the restaurant, which are the main evaluation requirements to influence the feeling time pressure food consumer to make decision whether he/she either still ought follow the better food taste, cheap food price factors to be preference decision or he/she ought follow short time queue time waiting or without queue time waiting, fast cooking waiting time factors to be preference restaurant consumption decision.

Hence, it seems that a feeling time pressure food consumer, he/she ought choose the restaurant to eat in preference when it does not need him/her to wait long queue time and wait long cooking time. Otherwise, when the food consumer does not feel hurry to eat, he/she outhgt choose the restaurant, it can provide good taste food, cheap price in preference to eat.

Hence, time pressure personal feeling will influence students or working people food consumers' preference restaurant choice when the restaurant can provide short time queue waiting or without queue waiting and fast cooking time service preference to satisfy their needs.

However , in some situation, time pressure can influence consumers to choose the service, even its price is expensive than other services. For example, public transportation tool choices service. When one passenger has need to find one kind public transportation tool to catch from the place to another destination, but the destination is far away from his/her location. He/she hopes to catch the kind of public transportation tool to arrive the destination about one hour. Although, his/her location has cheap public transportation tools to choose, e.g. bus, train, tram, ferry, underground train. But, he/she feels that all of these public transpotation tools need to spend longer time to compare taxi to arrive the destination. Although, these public transportation tools can be possible to arrive the destination withing one houe and they must charge cheaper fee to compare taxi. But, however the passenge hopes to arrive the destination in the shortest time. The most important influential factor is that the passenger feels personal time pressure to need to arrive the destination fastly and taxi public transportation tool is believed the fast transportation tool to arrive any destination to compare other general public transportation tools , when it has no traffic jam external environment factor influence. So, time pressure factor will influence passenger to choose taxi transportation tool in preference. Also, it seems that when the place often has many time pressure passengers are living. Then, the place's taxi business will be possible better than other locations. Hence, it implies that time pressure factor will bring need or demand number to be increased to some services.

Time pressure also influences how consumers choose to buy the kind of product, when he/she feels that the kind of product will be old fashin or it is not popular to use in society. For example, computer product, the traditional desktop large heavy weight computers will be possible to be replaced to use at home or office or any building places. Due to the laptop small light weight computers , it can be brought to anywhere by the users easily, even it can be brought to catch public transportation tool to use, it can be brought to restaurant, library, shopping centre etc. different public places to use conveniently. Due to some working people feel hurry to use computer to do their tasks, e.g. typing one document in short time. If they are not working in office and they have no computer on hand. They will worry about that they can not finish their tasks to give their bosses in limited time on the working day.

Hence, laptop computer will be one good chocie of task tool for busy working people when they need to often to use computer to finish urgent tasks in any time. Hence, it seems that the feeling time pressure working people will choose laptop computer in preference more than desktop traditional computer working tool. Due to the feeling time pressure workers, they feel that they can not finish their daily tasks in office. So, they will feel to need to use laptop computer task tool to help them to do office tasks . When they are catching transportation tool to go home or office time or lunch time , or holiday time. So, laptop computer product is more popular to time pressure working people target consumers.

Laptop computer products can also increase the feeling time pressure student consumers' needs. Because when one students feel home time is not enough to use computer to do their homeworkers at homes. When some students finish all lessons in schools and they need to catch public transportation tools to go home, in this catching public transportation time, they will be possible to hope to use one laptop computer to do their homeworks. So, one student who often feels time pressure to do whose homeworks, he will feel need to buy one laptop to carry it to anywhere, e.g. library, garden, school etc. different places. Then, he/she can do whom housework at any places in any time conveniently. Hence, it seems that their laptop computer products will be time pressure consumers' preference task tool.

In conclusion, the different factors influence consumer behaviors. Time pressure factor may be one main factor to influence consumers to choose to buy the kind of product or consume the kind of service in preference. So, when th consumer feels time presure to influence him/her to do preference choice to consume the kind of service of buy the kind of product. It is possible to occur to influence he/she does irrational economic choice decision. Hence, time pressure factor can being positive or negative both consumption emotion to some kinds of services or products . Hence, the increasing or decreasing number of consumers to some kinds of products or services, it has absolute relationship between of them. So, any product sellers or service providers can not neglect the importance of how time pressure factor influences consumer behavior in our nowadays society.

CHAPTER EIGHT

Time pressure impacts consumer behavioral effect

I shall indicate cases to explain that how time pressure environment factor impacts consumer behavior as well as what effects will be brought by time pressure consumer behavioral cause. Instead of above discussions concern how customer personal time pressure psychological factor influence, whether hoe time pressure environment factor will also influence consumer behavior. What are the difference between time pressure environment factor and time pressure consumer personal psychological factor? I shall explain as below:

Firstly, the impact of life satisfaction is caused by time pressure on consumers responses. Can effective advertising can impact of life satisfaction when the consumer feels need to buy the kind of product in any time pressure environment? Can effective advertising bring direct impact on sales when the consumer feels need to buy the kind of product in time pressure environment? Effective advertising may being advantages, includes customers feel easy to accept of price increases, favorable publicity, and reshaping market segmentation.

However, when the customer feels need life satisfaction in time pressure lif environment. The time pressure life environment ought impact on the consumer responses on advertising. Hence, when the consumer needs to live in the time pressure life environment. The over-commercialization of advertising ought impact the consumer chooses to buy the brand of product, when the seller has attractive advertising to bring purchase incentives to influence consumption desire to the time pressure environment influential consumer. For example, when the summer season will change to winter season, the ice cream consumers begins to feel weather will change to cold weather. Because many people feel more colf in the beginning. This is seasonable time pressure environment feeling, it may influence many ice-cream likers feel ice-cream may be possible shortage in hot weather or summer season, due to many ice-creams will be bought in summer weather to cause supermarkets in possible. So, if the brand ice-cream can make attractive advertisement to persuade ice-incream number will be reduced in the coming winter season beginning. So, it may influence many ice-cream likers choose to buy this brand's ice-cream in preference in summer. Because they feel fear none of any this brand's ice-creams can be sold in supermarkets in summer. Because they feel this brand's ice-cream , it's problem to let they can buy any different kinds of ice-cream taste to eat from any supermarkets in summer season. Hence, it explains why effective or attractive advertising may increase sale number, when consumers feel the brand's product number will be shortage or reduced from the seasonal time pressure external environment factor influence.

Secondly, I shall discuss what is the relationship between the effects of product popularity and time pressure on consumer responses? When a brand is popular to let many customers to familiarize in society. Does it increase time pressure to influence consumers choose in preference? Time pressure remaining to product popularity concerns how much sale number is raised to persuade consumers to choose to buy a preference for ecommerce online shopping. It seems to be one time pressure online sale environment. The effects of the ecommerce online shopping environment has relationship beteen pressure and product popularity on perceived risk and purchase intention.

In ecommerce online sale environment time pressure is operationized at the time remaining for consumers to sign up the online seller' website and property popularity is operationlized to the number of products already sold at the moment when consumers visit the web page. Hence, when on online consumer has intention to buy any products from internet. He/she will attempt to type the product name, then he/she will find some webpages which can provide the different brands of product photos, their prices informations to let the consumer to compare whether which brand of product price is more reasonable, better quality , good product image from the web pages' advertisement information to let him/her to evaluate. Hence, any product web page will influence how every online custmer feeling is good or bad to the web page's any brands of products. If the consumer feel the web page has many high product popularity indicators, it may bring a high consumption desire to let the online cusomer to evaluate the web page all prodocts in order to compare which brand of product is the best to choose to buy in time webpage view pressure consumption environment. Otherwise, if the consumer feels the web page has high product popularity indicator , it may bring a less consumption desire to let the online consumer to evaluate any of the webpage products to choose to buy. So, online webpage advertising information will be one time pressure online ecommerce consumption environment.

I assume that online shopping consumers won't like to stay to view on any webpage long time. It is possible that they choose to click more web pages to hope to find more different familiar and unfamiliar both brands of products informations in order to make more accurate comparison and evaluation from more different kinds of brands of products in order to make the most accurate online shopping decision. Hence, any brands of products online webpage information will be one time pressure limited sale environment to consumers feel that they need to make the most accurate online purchase decision in short time. Moreover, it seems that if the brand of products which can be showed on the popular product webpage, the it will have much sale chance to let online purchasers familiarize in order to increase sale opportunity more easily.

Finally, I shall explain what is the meaning of external time pressure consumption environment is the long time queue waiting consumption environment. I shall explain how to achieve one simplistic queueing system to solve long time queue waiting problem to bring consumers' negative emotion influence to choose to consume the service or buy the product in preference.

For entertainment service example, e.g. queueing at the cinema counter to buy one ticket to watch the movie , or queueing at the music hall to buy one ticket to listen the music performance show activities. The audiences' ticket purchase aims to sit down in the cinema or music hall to enjoy to listen and see pretty music performance or watch the attractive movie comfortable within one to two hours entertainment time. If the movie or music performance show is attractive, the cinema or music hall will have many audiences accept to spend long time to queue to buy the ticket. However, if the cinema ot music hall needs audience consumers to queue long time to buy the ticket, e.g. one houe , even more than one houe queueing time to wait to buy the ticket to watch the movie or listen the music performance show. Then, the long time queue waiting problem will be possible to cause a lot audiences number to be reduced, because they feel that they need to spend much time pressure to queue to by the ticket to listen the music performance show or watch the movie.

However, of these unacceptable too long queue time audiences can have another/ other cinema(s), music hall(s) to buy the same price , even more low price of movie ticket or music performance show ticket in short time. Then, they must leave the present cinema queue and go to the another cinema or music hall to buy ticket to watch the same movie or listen the same music performance show. So, long time queue is one external time pressure environment to influence consumer's preference choice to the service provider, when they feel it has another service provider does not need them or these audiences need to spend same long time queue time to wait to buy the ticket in order to enjoy the service, e.g. listening music performance show, watching movie.

Hence, in a high time pressure queue situation where decision makers, e.g. audiences have less time than needed (or perceived needed). It is very likely that they feel the queue waiting time stress of copying with themselves queue waiting time maximum limitation. So, if the movie ticket purchase audience feels that he/she will need to spend more than half hour to queue and half hour is himself/herself the maximum acceptable queue time level. So, his/her queue long time pressur negative emotion feeling will influence him/her to leave the cinema to choose another cinema. He/ she feels that ir does not need him/her to queue more than half hour in order to buy the ticket to watch the same movie in the another cinema, he/she can feel more comfortable to watch the movie. So, long time queue will influence some audiences choose aother service provider to replace it in possible short time, when they feel waiting in a queue is irritating, frustrating and hence costly.

What is a simplistic queueing system and how it can solve above queue problem. For a grocery store queueing counter case example, for one Apply brand computer shop example, the day's most busy queue time , there are about between fifty and hundred Apply brand potential computer buyers numbers every hour in the day. They need to queue to enquire the salespeople concern to any useful opinions to let them to know in order to make purchase decisions. But, the Apple brand computer shop lacks enough salespeople to answer their enquiries concern any computer purchase challenges. Every computer enquiry potential purchaser needs to spend at least half hour , even more time to queue to wait the salesperson to answer his/her enquiry in the counter queueing line. Hence, the feeling long time queue enquiry waiting consumers will feel time pressure to queue. Then, they will choose to leave the Apple brand computer shop's counter queue line. Consequently, the Apple brand computer will lose many potential computer buyers on the busy day.

The most simple solution is that it can increase the salespeople number in the most busy enquiry time every day. Hence, when every computer potential enquiry customer can contact every salesperson to listen whom opinion concerns his/her any computer enquiry issues in order to let he/she feels that they every one can provide excellent sale service computer issues enquiry explanation performance to satisfy his/her enquiry need to let himself/herself to feel in the short enquiry time. Due to they do not need to spend long queue time to wait every salesperson's feedback or opinion to solve their enquiries in the computer shop. Because they do not feel presure to spend long time to queue to wait the computer shops's every salesperson's opinion. So, they will raise satisfactory feeling to thie Apple computer shop's every salesperson individual sale enquiry service performance.

Consequently, the day's computer sale number will be possible to raise after the salespeople can spend much time to solve their enquiries effectively and efficiently.

● The reasons cause consumers feel
time pressure

What factors can cause consumers feel time pressure to but the product in the personal time limited dominated consumption environment? It is one interesting question: Why does the consumer feel time pressure to make short time purchase decision making? I shall indicate some cases to explain this possibility as below:

First, I shall indicate household purchaser time pressure consumption behavior. Consumer house buyer behavior, some house buyer will feel personal time pressure to choose the different houses to make house purchase decision in short time. For example, if the house developer has a 30% discount house price to sell only in the short three months. So, after this three months, all house purchaser will need to pay the original house price. If the house developer's houses prices are between US doller one million to two million every house. For one million house price after 30% discount , the house buyer only needs to pay seventy million. For two million house price after 30 % discount, the house buyer only needs to pay one hundred and fourty million. So, expensive product's financing factor will influence the buyer's consumption time pressure, such as the house discount price case, due to the house developer's houses prices are very expensive. However, if any house buyers can make decisin to buy its houses in three months. Then, they can pay les 30% of the houses prices. Such as the original price one million house, the house buyer can pay less thirty million amount or the original price two million houses prices. The house buyer can pay less sixty million amount. So, the large discount financing amount may be attractive purchase method to influence many house buyers feel time pressure to decide whether they ought choose to buy the property developer's houses in these three months. It is one short term cheap house financing price to let many house buyers feel time pressure to make house purchase decision from this house developer in these three months . Hence, short term high discount price to expensive product financing factor will influence consumers feel it is right time to make pressure consumption decision.

Hence, such as this three months house discount price case, when the property buyer gain this property developer's knowledge of three months house discount price message. This sudden three months house discount price message will be one attractive knowledge of factor to impact the potential property buyers' house purchase desires to be raised in three months time pressure house purchase consumption environment. So, it is one feeling sudden time pressure consumption desire good example for this three monts large discount attractive houes price to influence house buyers to make house purchase decision from the house developer in these three months. Consequently, house developer will have possible to raise the large house sale number , if this 30 % house discount price can let many property buyers feel it is one worth purchase price in these three months. So, they will consider that they can not pay less 30% discount price to buy this house developer's any houses after three months. So they need to make house purchase decision in these three months short term time pressure house consumption market for this property developer.

So, this time pressure financing advantage will only bring benefit to this property developer, this time pressure financing advantage won't bring benefit to other property developers, because all property buyers feel need to make property purchase decision in these three months suddenly, due to this property developer can provide a special 30 discount price to any property final decision making to choose to buy its houses in these three months temporary short time. It seems that three months short time can cause final house purchase choice time pressure to any potential property buyers. They expect to gain high discount price to buy any expensive houses. So, these expenaive house potential buyers will feel need to make final expensive house purchase decision to choose to buy this property developer's expensive houses in these final three months perios. So, time pressure can occur in any short period, when the seller can provide any special sale promotion to persuade consumers to feel need to make sudden time pressure that purchase decision is they hope to earn special sale promotion consumption in the short limited sale perios for the seller.

Hence, consumer personal time pressure feeling, it can be predictive to any time occurrence pychological consumption, feeling, such as the property developer's sudden high per cent discount price to expensive house less dinancing burden factor to influence the expensive house buyers feel that whether they ought do choice house purchase decision in these short term three months , because the house developer's unpredictive and sudden attractive expensive houses reducing prices strategy. So, this property developer's short term three months high house discount price time pressure consumption strategy may persuade or attract , even encourage many potential expensive house buyers choose to spend lesser amount to buy this property developer's discount houses, either is paid by house mortgage bank loan lending payment method or installment payment method or on-time all payment method. So, the different house payment choice buyers will be influenced to make immediate property purchase decision in these three months time pressure period from this property developer's expensive discounted house number influence.

However, in this house market time pressure consumption environment, the property developer's expensive house supply number may also have influential effort to excite the expensive house buyers' house purchase consumption desires, for example, if the other expensive house property developers' between US one million and US two million of every property price's these houses in the country's property marker totel suppy number is one thousand property unit number. The potential property buyers , they plan to buy these amounts of expensive houses , the property needers estimate three thousand buyers number at least. Hence, it seems that these expensive house buyers' demand id more than three times to expensive property supply number.

Moreover, the other property developer's expensive property developers ' expensive house prices have no any discount in this three months periods, and some property developers' expensive house prices tend to increase 1 to 10 per cent in these three months period. Hence if the property developer can supply at least three thousand property units number between US one million and US two million sale price and all of these expensive houses are reduced 30 per cetnt discount to sell in these three months .

Consequently, it is possible to persuade all estimated three thousand expensive house potential buyers choose to buy this property developer's houses in these three months in possible. So, it explain that why this property developer's expensive discounted house supply number will influence these property buyers' preference choice. If this property developer has only one thousand expensive houses to be supplied by discounted 30% sale price. Then, it will cause shortage of expensive houses to satisfy these three thousand expensive house buyer estimated number in the country in three month discount sale promotion period.

Consequently, this property developer will lose two thousand these prices of expensive house potential buyers number in all these three months discounted sala period . I assume that all these three thousand expensive house property buyers will be influenced to make choice to buy its all dicounted expensive houses in these three month time pressure discounted sale period. So, it needs to do data gather concerns how many of thee expensive house potential house buyers number in its country in order to avoid discounted expensive houses supply number to cause shortage supply challenges and bring these expensive house potential buyers lose number in these three months period.

In conclusion, it explains why that supply number will influence this property developer's sale number in these three months sale period. Consequently, time pressure sale strategy ans supply number has close relationship to influence the seller's sale number in the time pressure sale period.

Secondly, I shall discuss how does environment time pressure factor influences consumer behavior? Does time pressure influence consumer donating behavior? I assume that external environment time pressure factor can influence consumer changes whom original purchase decision making. What circumstance's time can influence consumer individual to feel time pressure to consume. For example, when the consumer expects have one hour to choose whether which brand of product to buy among the different kinds of products. The circumstance is changed suddenly. It influences the consumers feel that they has only 10 minutes to make the final purchse decision.

Why does the consumer feel enough brand of product? What external circumstance factors influence he/she feels only 10 minutes time to make the final purchase decision suddenly? For travel fair time limited external environment influential pressure travelling consumption case example, the international travel fair can indicate that time limited pressure has positive significant influence on traveller perceived value and purchase intention in short time. In addition, perceived value is served as a mediating factor between the relationship of time limited pressure and feeling travelling entertainment purchase intention to the travel fair visitors. It has a beneficial reference for planning a travelling show or fair marketing strategy.

One attractive travelling fair/show can promote the country's different attractive travelling destinations to let the travellinf show's visitors to know. It can particularly influence the visitors' long time travelling planning , it can be shorten be short time travelling planning, e.g. after one year's travelling planning can be influenced to make immediate focused on choosing the country's travelling decision if he/she feels the country has more attractive travelling destinations, he/she prefers to go to travel in short time, e.g. within 6 months . So, when the travelling exhibition fair/ show can provide the country's beautiful scene photos to let the visitors to view. Then, it will bring effective time pressure feeling to let some travelling visitos feel travelling needs immediately in the travelling exhibition show/ fair . This travelling exhibition show/fair can bring the time limited pressure benefit. It is as an external environment factor that can influence the travelling visitors' travelling desires to be raised , when they can view many benefitical scene photos of the country' different undiscovered travelling destination . Then, it can increase their travelling desires to the country in possible.

I shall explain why travelling exhibition show/fair can play an important role in travelling consumer perceived quality and travelling country destination choice decision making to influence travelling visitors feel time limited pressure. However, perceived value has been show to be a value has been shown to be a value of perceived quality and perceived sacrifice to cause travelling visitors feel more interesting to choose to travel the country when they can view the attractive beautiful scence photos in the travelling exhibition show/fair.

A successful travelling exhibition show/fair can bring time limited process increases , the travelling visitors pay more attention to key travelling destination features and positive travelling information from the scene photos and travelling destinations introduction. So , the country's attractive travelling destinations scene photos and clear travelling introduction to different destinations information will be important message to let the different countries' travelling visitors to know when they spend a limited time to enter the travelling exhibition show/fair to view the different scene photos . If the travelling visitor feel very satisfied to the country's travelling exhibition show/fair. Then, this travelling exhibition excite whom travelling interest to choose to go to the country to travell in short time, when the travelling visitors are influenced to feel the country has many beautiful destinations where they feel have travelling interest in the limited time pressure travelling exhibition show/fair environment. If the travelling exhibition show/fair needs they to pay enter fee and it has only two hours or less time to premit to stay in the travelling exhibition show/fair.

Hence, if the time pressure limited travelling exhibition show/fair can let the travelling visitors feel attractive and enjoyable view feeling when they look every the country's any scene beautiful photos and indication how to the different travelling destinations and explains why the country's travelling places are value travelling destinations to let the exhibition visitors to know, when they do not know or discover these any one of value travelling places in the country before. Then, this limited time staying travelling exhibition show/fair will bring positive time pressure to influence some travelling visitors feel interesting to visit the country's inknown or undiscovery travelling destinations in short time. So, all attractive travelling exhibition shows/fairs are one external environment time limited positive pressure factor to excite some travelling visitors' travelling desires in short time in possible.

Instead of travelling exhibition show/fair can bring external environment positive limited time positive pressure to excite travelling visitors' travelling consumption desires, the another external environment positive limited time positive pressure case is that mobile coupons of limited mobile phone sale number or discount mobile phone call payment plan in short time case. How and why mobile coupons can excite any mobile consumption and/ or mobile phone call user choice to the mobile phone sale company or mobile phone call service provider.

An effective mobile plane useful limited time beneficial purchase strategy can encourage some mobile phone consumers to choose to use the brand mobile useful phone call service plan immedicately. if the mobile phone call service plan is attractive to the mobile phone call consumer . For example, dynamic discounts strategies are used by marketers to send scaraity message which lead to higher consumers' mobile phone purchase intention. An utility increasing discount straregy provides mobile phone call users with an increasing discount over time (e.g. 30% discount for in-store consumption for 30 minutes, after which the discount increases to 40 % , an utility discount strategy provides the same discounts for mobile phone call users over a specific promotional period (e.g. 40% discount from 9AM to 5 PM) phone call using time. An utility decreasing discount strategy offers mobile phone call users with a decreasing discount over time (e.g. 40% discount for in -store consumption for 10 minutes, after which the discount decreases to 30%).

However, these three different discount strategies for bargaining have different impacts on outcomes. However, they have same influences to lead mobile phone call users feel time pressure to do choose whether this mobile phone call using plan is suitable. If the mobile phone call user feels this mobile phone call using plan is suitable to use, then this mobil coupon promotion strategy can influence mobile phone user feels limited time pressure to persuade him/her to choose to use its mobile phone call service under different time limitation, quantity limitation and discount strategies on the mobile phone user's mobile phone call plan using intention.

Furthermore, I hypothesize that the brand of mobile phone quantity, limited scarcity message that gives a perception that the brand of any kinds of mobile phones are limited for purchase, it will have a positive impact on mobilt phone consumers' perceived value of mobile products, leading to a greater tendancy to make mobile phone purchase decision immediately. Hence, mobile coupon is one type of price-incentive promotion. In various price incentives, discount strategy is a mode of price negotiation between the mobile product conumer and the merchant, such as the mobile phone seller , mobile phone call user and mobile phone call service provider.

However, mobile coupons offer discount under a time constraint to induce perceived scarcity. Scarce commodities are more attractive than those with plenty inventory due to the speciality and uniqueness of the former perceived by the consumer. However, scarcity has both forms. They incluce quantity scaracity can let consumers feel need to buy the product in short time. Otherwise, due to stock shortage or low inventory to influence they can not brought the kind of product. Time scarcity means products are for sale only for a designated

CHAPTER NINE

May time dominate consumption final purchase decision making

Whether can time limited pressure dominate consumer individual to make more rational purchase decision? Can the consumer make more rational decision , when he/she has enough time to make final purchase decision? I shall explain why and how the consumer can make more rational decision when he/she has enough time as well as I shall explain that without time pressure environment. It may dominate consumers to make more rational or more accurate decision making.

I assume that it is the final time limited pressure day to nee the consumer to spend more nervous do time final purchase decision among the different kinds of similar products choices, e.g. air conditions . If the consumer decides that the day is the final purchase decisin to choose to buy one air conditin among these different brands of similar air conditions in the super store. So, if on the that day, he/she can not make any final decisin to choose which brand of air condition to buy on that final consumption day in the super store when the super store visitor sees the final air condition consumption day advertisement in this year in this super store . Then, he/she won't buy any air condition again if he/she can not buy on that day in this super store.

The another time dominates immediate purchase behavior is that I assume that one common air condition can not be bought in short time later if all air condition consumers can not make decision to buy any air condition in this super store. So, his/her personal time limited pressure can dominate whose final or condition purchase decision in this super store on that day. If the store has many different brands of air conditions to lead him/her to spend long time to compare which is th best worth to buy in this super store. Then, it will let him/her to feel difficult to make the air condition final purchase decision in the store on that day. Otherwise, if the super store has less different brands of air conditions to need him/her to spend less time to compare which is the best worth to buy in the store. Then, he/she may make the final air conditin purchase decision making more easily on that day.

So, the final air condition purchase day of the super store, the super store's air condition final day's time can dominate the air condition buyer to make air condition purchase decision immediately. Due to he/she feels that all of these day brands air conditions can not bought from this super store after that day. So, he/she needs to make the air condition purchase decision making in this super store on that final air condition purchase day in this year. Because it is the final air condition purchase day in this super store of all sir conditions products. If he/she can not make the choice to buy any one brand of air condition in this store. Then, it is possible that he/she will lose this store's final cheap price air condition purchase benefits. However, if this super store has too many brands of air conditions need him/her to choose. It will cause him/her to spend more time to choose. Consequently, it will cause he/she feels difficult to compare which brand of air condition is the best and he / she does not choose to buy any one in this super store.

Hence, this super store ought have less number different brands of air conditions to let every air condition consumer to choose in order to let they can make final air condition purcahse decision on this air condition cheap price purchase final day. So, less different number brands of air conditions will dominate the consumers to spend less time to make purchase decision immediately and easily on that final sale day in this super store. Hence, it seems that the super store's final air conditions sold day time will dominate many air condition visitors to make purchase decision when they visit this super store in summer season on that day in this super store. Because all this super store's air condition consumers do not expect that they can not buy the best quality of air conditin in this super store final sold day , due to air condition stocks number shorten challenge is not supplied enough on that final cheap purchase day in this super store. Consequently, that time pressure will increase to influence them to make the final air condition purchase decision in the final sold day' s short time, before this super store closing time on that day. Their time pressure feeling comes from the super store 's air condition number shortage supply in possibility. It will dominate them to make the final air condition purchase decision in this super store in short time.

The anothe time dominates immediate purchase behavior case is that I assume that one common picture painter(actor), he finds one architect to help him to build one house. The architect only needs to folloe his house picture to build one house. The common picture painter tells him that he will give him building expenditure and building profit after he helps him to build the house profit after he helps him to build the house successfully. After six months, the architect made one decision, he did not demand the famous picture painter paid him for the building service fee. But, he needed him give the house picture to him to replace the building service fee. Because the picture painter feels that he didn't need to pay the building service fee to him to buy the architect's building service in these six months building time. Hence, he accepted his offer to give his common house picture to the architect for his reward.

I assume that this six months time dominate the architect to make the final building service fee decision either acceptance the common picture painter customer's building service fee or acceptance his common house picture replaces the building service fee. However, the architect believes that this common house picture can have higher selling price to compare his building service fee income. Consequently, I assume that his evaluation is right, this house picture selling price is more than three times to compare his past six months's building service income. So, it proved that his choice is right, because he could earn more than three times of his building service income after he decided to accept the common picture painter's this house picture to attempt to sell it in the picture auction market. It seems that this six months long house building time can dominate these both buyer and seller's purchase and selling behaviors, such as this picture painter and this architect. When the architect has this six months enough time to let the picture painter to change his building service offer decision from building service fee payment to his common house picture offer exchange. This architect can achieve his intention to let him to accept his free house picture sold product exchange offer more easily. Otherwise, if the architect can not need six months to build this house, he only needs three months or less time to build this house, then it is possible that the picture painter won't accept his this house picture offer to replace his building service fee easily. If he considers that whether his this house picture's selling price has possible to sell higher price to compare this building service fee for this house picture. He will choose to sell this house picture himself. Hence, due to the picture painter can not sell this house picture in this past six months. So, in this six months period, the house painter can not sell this house picture in picture auction market. This six months period can dominate his low market worth selling feeling to this house picture as well as it can influence him to make this house picture exchange decision to replace his house service fee.

The picture painter will ask himself, ought the house picture painter need to wait how long time to sell this picture in auction market, because he does not know whether the architect needs how long time to build this house? So, this house building time can dominate the picture painter's acceptance of the architect's this free house picture product exchange offer, which is easier acceptance or difficult acceptance . In this six month' house building period between the architect service provider and the picture painter house buyer. Hence,the house building time can dominate the house building provider and the picture painter's house building buyer both's house picture free exchange purchase change behavioral choice between of them influentially.

The another time dominates consumption behavior case is that time rich or time poor factor, e.g. one fast food famous restaurant , its success is not only due to its fast food good taste factor, its restaurant location whether is close to the time poor people's offices, it is one main factor. Because this fast food famous restaurant only choose to build its restaurants to close to offices in any large cities in different countries. Hence, the franchisees need to pay expensive franchise loyalty income to buy its franchise in order to it can supply fast foods to the franchisees to sell, but they also need to pay expensive rent to this fast food franchiser, due to their fast food restaurant locations has been chose to locate in the main cities in different countries from the fast food famous restaurant's location decision. Hence, whether long or short time fast restaurant rent period to the franchisees , which can dominate the fast food restaurants's royalty and rent income. For example, if one fast food franchisee only sign one year contract to buy the fast food franchisor's loyalty to help it to sell its fast foods only one year, because it does not ensure how many fast food consumers will choose to buy these fast foods to eat, due to its price is decided by the fast food franchisor. If the cities have other fast food restaurants to let them to choose, they may find other fast food restaurants to replace it to eat fast foods very easily.

If this fast good restaurant is not the most famous and it operates only short time. So, it can not earn more fast food franchisees' confidence to accept to pay long time rent to operate its fast food restaurants in cities and pay long time royalty fee to it. Otherwise, if the fast food restaurant had operated its restaurant for a long time period to raise its fast food loyalty's to let many different countries' fast food eaters to familiarize or acknowledg its fast food brand in popular. So, long fast food opersation time can confirm that it has many fast food eaters, they prefer to choose to eat its fast foods. It can increase the franchisees' confidence to choose to rent its fast food restaurants and pay royalty to it in preference. Hence, the fast food franchisor's restaurant operation time whether it is long or short time, this franchisor's fast food restaurant operating time pressure factor will dominate the fast food franchisees' choices to decide to pay how long rent sand franchise royalty income to rent its restaurant to do the franchisee's fast food business in the cities locations in different countries. So, it seems that the fast food franchisor's business operation time can dominate the frahchisees' choice.

In special , in fast food industry, time rich and time poor consumers behavior will dominate their fast food choices. Time rich people feel they have enough or too much time when time poor people feel time is a major constraint in their daily life. The explansion of the fast food business, and the increase eatting of fast food are indicators of this trend. At the same time, shorter working hours increased wealth and less pressure on domestic rountines have opened up new segments of leisure consumption. But, " free time" in certain areas has not for many people, lead to an increases feeling of time richness.

So, it explains that why many fast food consumers who feel not enough time to work daily. They are time poor working people usually. So, instead of fast food taste factor influences consumer number. The people who feel time rich or poor, e.g. employmet rich or poor lunch time to the employee, it will dominate the employee chooses to go to fast food restaurant in preference. So, the fast food restaurant can supply rich time to let them to eat lunch in short time, if the employee has less time to eat lunch or more tasks need hime to do on that day afternoon. Hence, feeling time rich or poor to the people factor, which will dominate some consumers' choices to some kinds of businesses, such as fast food industry, or for public transportation tool choice case example, one time poor passenger feels need to go to the destination in short time. The time poor passenger will prefer to choose taxi in preference, then it is possible train or underground train, next it is tram, fainally, it is bus or ferry public transportion tool choices. Otherwise, for one time rich passenger, he has more time to go to the destinaton. The time rich passenger will prefer to choose the cheap public transportation tool , such as bus, ferry, underground train, ferry, train. The final choice is taxi. So, passenger's time pressure will influence whose public transportation tool choice.

● Time pressure dominiates consumer psychological factor

What are the factors of time pressure dominate consumer purchcase psychological behaviors? How any why do this time pressure psychological factors dominate consumer behaviors? It is possible that time pressure can dominate consumer mind and behavior either choose to buy the product/ consume the service or not buy the product/consume the service. Every consumer's final purchase decision, he/she is influenced how to make by himself/herself personal psychological limited time pressure . It means that he/she will have one time maximum standard to demand himself/herself to make the final purchase decision in whose individual psychological time standard (the consumer's individual psychological limited consumption time). So, it seems that ever consumer's final decision how he/she chooses to buy the product or consume the service, his/her consumption behavior will be dominated by whose psychological time limited consumption pressure.

So, time pressure issue seems evolutionary psychology, it looks at how consumer behavior has beed affected by psychological adjustments during time pressure evoluation. It seeks to identify which consumer psychological traits are evolved through adaptations, e.g. time pressure consumption adaptations to choose the final purchase decision in the final time limited consumption pressure environment, e.g. the consumer expects this day is the final day to choose to buy what kinds of the product. If he/she can't make final purchase decisin on the day, he/she will choose to buy the kind of product later, even he/she does not choose to buy the kind of product in the first or again, that is the products of natural selection, or the supermaket visitor case, he expects to choose which kind of food to eat within final 15 minutes, if he/she can't make the final decision to buy what kind of food to eat within final 15 minutes in this supermarket , or the restaurant eatting consumer case, he is queueing to wait to enter the restaurant to eat. He/ she expects the final queue waiting time is 15 minutes maximum. If after this 15 minutes, he/she can not be permitted to enter this restaurant, then he/she will choose to leave this restaurant and he/she will find another restaurant to replace it. So, it seems that any consumer will have himself/ herself consumption limited stardard time to decide whether he/she ought choose to buy any products or consume any services in any consumption environment.

Hence, the cause of consumption time pressure dominates consumer behavior, it is based on these hypothesis: Every consumer has demand characteristic and time pressure can dominate how he/she make final decision to buy or not buy any product or consume any service as well as any consumer needs have time pressure consumption demand because he/ she does not expect to epend more time to choose what kinds of products to buy or what kinds of services to consume. He/she expects to make purchase or consumption final decision in short time.

IN fact, consumers will be encoded to influence how they make final purchase decision. There are three main ways in which product information can be encoded. They include: Visual (product picture) ; for example, the conumer stores the memory by visualizing it as on product image. Aconstic (sound); here the consumer stores the information as a sound , this explains why some consumers sometimes get the brand name(words) that sound the same mixed up when they try to remember them. Semantic (meaning); here the object is stored in terms of what it means rather than as an image or sound, e.g. when the brand of toys can let many children feel fun to play. Then, when many parents feel familiar to the toy brand, they must remember this toy brand company is selling any kinds of toys to let children to play. So, famous brand can let consumers familiarize what products that it is selling. Such as the toy brand company can let parents feel its toys are fun to let their children to play. All these sensory information can dominate consumers make final choice purchase behavior to buy its product or consume its service in preference in any time limited pressure environment, if the brand can give positive information memory to let many customers to remember.

So, it seems that consumers are dominated to choose which kinds of products to buy or which kinds of services to consume by positive or negative emotion, time pressure in any consumption environment immediately. It is one time pressure consumption environment theory factor, it can influence consumer behavior is changed in any consumption environment time. Consequently, it explains that why time pressure can dominate consumer behaviors in possible. Also, any product seller or service provider needs to consider how to manage consumption time process to be longer to cause its consumers doe not choose to buy its product or consume its service consequently.

CHAPTER TEN

Methods avoid consumers feel time pressure

In business society, it seems that any consumers will feel time pressure to cause their purchase decision making process changes in any consumption suitations, when they feel time pressure either by themselves or third parties influence, e.g. not buying any thing, not consuming any service, irrational making consumption final decision etc. consumption behaviors. How to reduce their time pressure to avoid they do above consumption behaviors. I shall indicate some consumption suitations to explain how to avoid their reducing consumption , due to time pressure factor influences as below:

Firstly, I shall indicate supermarket consumption environment example. In general, supermarket visitors will expect to spend less time to visit any supermarkets to make choice to biy any foods. They will stay short time when they expect to buy less foods, even, they will stay more short time when they expect to buy more less foods in any supermarkets. So, any supermarkets will need to calculate their clients' limited time pressure how to influence their foods consumption number. If the supermarket visitor expects to spend maximum 20 minutes to buy any foods in the supermarket. Then, he may choose some different kinds of foods to buy, e.g. icecream, fruit, bread, jam, fish etc. different kinds of foods, Otherwise, if the another supermarket visot expects to spend maximum 10 minutes to buy any foods in the supermarket. Then, he may choose less different kinds of foods to compare the first one, e.g. fish, jam, icecream only or bread, fruit , jam only. So, the second one supermarket visitor will buy less different kinds of foods, because he expects to spend 10 minutes maximum , his shopping spending time is less 10 minutes to compare the first one supermarket visitor. Because different supermarket visitor personal time pressure will limit him/her to choose more or less different kinds of foods to buy. However, time pressure will not influence every kind of foods number because every kind of food purchase number will not be influenced to buy more or less , due to the supermarket visitor personal time pressure variable factor influences his/her foods purchase number. Otherwise, the different kinds of food choice will be influenced to choose to either buy or not buy , due to every supermarket visitor personal time pressure is different.

Hence, supermarkets can focus on how to avoid any kinds of food purchase choice loses , due to supermarket consumer personal time pressure influences. In fact, in supermarket every shelf, it usually has many different brands of every kind of foods to let supermarket visitors to choose to buy. For example,the kind of jam food number has many brands are placed on shelf to let them to choose, e.g. there are more than 10 different brands of jam food are placed on one shelf. It will bring one choice problem. IF one supermarket visitor expects to choose one brand of jam within 5 minute, then he finds the shelf has more than 10 different brands of jam are placed on the shelf. Then he will feel time pressure to cause difficulty to choose the best brand of jam to buy from these 10 brands of jam. It will bring the negative emotion if he feels that all of these 10 brands of jam taste and price has no more difference. Consequently, these 10 brands of jam choice will cause he can not make the final jam purchase decision within this 5 minutes individual time limited. Anyway, if there are only 5 brands of jam are placed on this shelf, then the 5 minutes time limited consumer will has less brands of jam choices, it will influence him to do more easy choice to buy one kind of brand jam food from the shelf. It is one limited time pressure of psychological choice factor to influence any consumers feel to do any brand of food choice more easy in short time. Hence, I recommend supermarket shelf ought place every kind of food brand maximum to 5 brands , it is the best food brand number to every supermarket's shelves to let any consumers to choose different kinds of foods to make the easy food choice way in supermarket food market.

So, in super store market, it is similar to supermaket market. Super stores' main products are cloths, shoes, bags, stationarys, electronic products, e.g. fans, air conditions, televisons, radios, warmers, washing machines, dry machines, computers etc. However, super store visitors will like to spend more time to stay in any super stores, due to they feel to need more time to make purchase decision in order to make the most right choice to buy these any products. They usually expect to stay half hour , even one hour or more time in super stores. Their time pressures are depended on whether what kinds of products that they expect to buy in the super store. For example, if the super store visitor expects to buy one laptop computer. He will expect to make purchase choice decision within half hour, even more time. Otherwise, if the super store visitor expects to buy stationery, e.g. pen and rubber and pencil, he will expect to make purchase choice decision within 10 minutes. So, when the super store visitor expects to buy the product is more expensive, then his time pressure time will be longer than the super store visior expects to buy the product is cheap, such as stationery and laptop two kinds of products.

However , due to super store 's expensive and cheap product consumers whose time pressures are different. So, brands choice number will have much different between them. For laptop example, due to superstore visitors can accept to spend longer time to make laptop purchase choice. So, one shelf can place 5 to 10 different brands of laptops , another shelf can place 5 to 10 different brands of laptops to let them to choose. Otherwise, for stationery example, due to superstore visitors can not accept to spend longer time to make stationery purchase choice. so, one shelf can place less than 5 brands of pens, the another shelf can place less than 5 brands of pencils or another shelf can place less than 5 brands of rubbers , another shelf can place less than 5 brands of rulers to let them to make purchase choice in short time.

Secondly, for restaurant eaters example, when one restaurant has many eaters choose to enter this restaurant to eat its food, then it only chooses to let some eaters to enquire ticket number to queue to wait. Of course, some eaters will not like to wait too long time, so they will leave the queue to choose another restaurant to replace it in possible. For example, in afternoon eating time, these are two busy eaters, the student feels hurry to go to school or the working person feels hurry to go to office after lunch, although the restaurant service staff had given him one ticket to let them to queue to wait. However, their expected queue waiting time is within 15 maximum, but there are many eaters are queuing and their ticket numbers are small numbers. So, they feel that they must not enter this restaurant within 15 minutes themselves limited queue time. Consequently, their late entering this restaurant after 15 minutes issue will influence that they will choose another restaurant in possible. So, the restaurant long time queue will cause some eaters choose another restaurant in busy time. I recommend that the restaurant can limit every eater's eatting time, e.g. it calculate every eater's restaurant entering time and it limits every must leave the restaurant within half hour in busy eatting time. It can post notice to let them to know in the front door, e.g. Every eater needs to leave our restaurant within half hour, otherwise, you will need to bring your food to leave please. So, every eater know that they need to eat all food within half hour, otherwise, they need to bring their food to leave this restaurant. Then, this restaurant can increase more seats to let many queue waiting eaters , they do not queue to spend long time to wait to enter this restaurant. Consequently, many queue waiting eaters will choose to enter this restaurant, due to their queue waiting times are not exceed their time pressure limited time.

The final case is cinema queue . In general, any cinemas will have many audiences need to wait to buy tickets to watch movies. However, if the cinema has many audiences , they need to spend one hour, or two hours , even more than two hours to queue to wait to buy the ticket to watch any movies in the cinema. If some audiences' expected queue waiting times are within one hour. So, if these audiences' expected queue waiting timesa are more than one hour. Then, they will choose to leave this cinema and choose other cinemas to replace it in possible. How to avoid these time pressure audiences losing number increases in cinema busy time? I recommend that this cinema ought increase ticket purchase counter service staffs number , e.g. opening more three to five ticket purchase counters number in order to let these one hour time queue time waiting audiences can purchase ticket to watch their movies within one hour. So, opening urgent ticket purcahse service counters number issue is depended on whether there are how many audiences are waiting to buy ticket in the cinema in the time. However, it is only one best way to avoid the cinema audiences number loses in cinema busy time.

CHAPTER ELEVEN

Time press how influences video playing game consumer purchase behavior

I shall explain that why it has relationship between the video game student consumer individual learning time and the working people individual working time both can influence video game playing consumer individual video game choice behavior. I shall assume that the different kinds of video game content difficult or easy win competition and entertainment spending on playing time factor will have more influence how the student or working person individual choice of what kind of video game purchase. Otherwisem evey video game price and brand and video game entertainment design content will have less inflience to every video game consumer individual purchase choice.

Why do the every video game's learning playing time and the playing time is spent to satisfy the feeling of winning game both factors will be the main factors to influence the feeling busy learning student or feeling rest working personal target video game playing consumer individual kind of which video game software purchase choice? Why do feeling busy learning students or feeling rest working people will be prefer to choose to buy the kinds of need spending little time to learn to play to achieve the easy winning of the video game content aim in short time?

Nowadays, the different brands of video game products have different prices, various entertainment design contents and the easy or difficult win content feeling to be promoted to sell to satisfy the students or working people video game players' entertainment needs. However, time pressure will be one important factor to influence students of working peoples' video games choices. I shall explain that the time pressure factor how will influence the feeling busy learning or feeling rest working video game players or video game content software consumers to choose to buy the kinds of video games softwares which can let them to feel to spend little playing and learning time and they can feel easy to win the the video game competition in short time preference in this electronic enterainment video game industry.

Nowadays, video game target customers, they are young students and adult working people in common. When , the student does not need to go to school and he/she stays at home, he /she will like to play video game after he/she finishs to learn just a moment usually or the adult working person finishs jobs on the day, after he/she ate dinner, he/she will also like to play video game at home. So , video game can be one kind of entertainment product to let they feel enjoy to play when they re staying at homes.

Video game can be one kind of entetaiment culture or entertainment behavior at home to them in popular. A player's ability to perform within a game entertainment is important, and players tend to knowledgeable about their achievements and failures within any game world. So, when one student hopes toget pass grade in school examination. He will choose to spend little time to attempt to win the video game content competition in short time because it can let him to feel that may increase his confidence to pass the grade in the school examination later in possible when he ensures that he had won the video game content competition. He believes that he can be trained to raise whose judgement and mind and analysis abilitiy in his playing visdo game proceed. Instead of playing video game can increase student learning confidence, it can also increase the working people's confidence, when the working person hopes to be promoted or increased salary later from his supervisor's appreciation. He will attempt to spend little time to win the kind of video game content competition in short time. He will have more condifent to achieve to raise his working performance to let his supervisor appreciation if he can learn how to win the kind of video game competition in short time.

It seems that whether the player needs to spend how much time to learn how to win any kind of video content game competitin , this " spending learning time of winning any video content game competition in time pressure playing environment feeling factor will influence the student or working person 's video game content purchase choice. If the video game design is more complex or difficult to let the player to feel to learn to win the game competition as well as it also needs them to spend more long time to learn to play and win the kind of video content game competition. Then, it has possible to influence the hard learning students or hard working people video game consumers, they do not choose to buy any kinds of need spending long learning and playing time to win the kinds of video content game competitive software products. So, it seems that the spend how much playing and learning time to win the video game content competition factor will bring time pressure to let the hard working people or hard learning student video game consumers choose to buy the video content game software products are easy to learn to play in preference because they expect to pass grade or appreciate easy, if they feel that they can learn how to win the video game content competition in short time as well as they do not spend much playing time to win the kind of video game content competition and they will reduce their learning time at homes.

I shall explain why price won't be the main factor to influence video game players' purchase choices in preference. Some video game software sellers feel reduced sale price can attract many video game buyers' choice in preference. It is one wrong mind, due to video game software price is not too much high, it is one kind popular cheap entertainment software product. So , the kinds of similar entertainment content design video game products , their sale price difference between the kind of most expensive , the highest price video game software and the kind of the cheapest , the lowest price video game software won't be difference very much. Their price difference level may be US 410 to US$50 or even less than US$50 level. So,, one video fame entertainment player won't feel that the kind of similar content design of video game software's higher price which will influence he chooses to buy another cheaper similar of kind video game content design software product to replace to the prior higher price one. Because their price difference are not too much or video game software entertainment product is not on kind of expensive product to let them to feel. So, it seems what video game software price won't influence the video game players' prior one of preference choice, it is not easy to be replaced from later cheaper one, when the video game player feels like to play the kind of high price of video game content software before.

Can the video game content influence player individual purchase motivation in preference? In fact, there are many different kinds of video game contents to let players to choose. This free-to -play busines model that has rapidly speed to achieve games services to general . So, some students or working people players can free download some kinds of video game softwares to play from online channel. It will be attractive to the no paid video game players. Hence, free download video game content will influence the paid video game players' purchase decisions for in -game content are not only affected by people's existing general attitudes, consumption values, and movitations , but also by the design decisions and the needs built into the game by the developers. Because the paid video game players won't like to buy the similar content video games, which can be free download to play from online or internet channel. They will feel infair or not worth or loss if they choose to pay to buy the similar video game content entertainment software, after they discovered that they may be free download this kind of similar video game content to play from internet.

It will bring this question: Why will time pressure influence video game player chooses to download free video game to play in preference? When one student feels that he has no enough time to study, he won't choose to fo to any video game shops to do video game software comparative behavior to compare which one's price is lower, game playing content is more attractive, brand is familar in order to make final purchase decision in preference. If he discovered that there has one kind of video game content, which can be free download to play from internet or online channel . So, when the student feels that he needs have much time to study on the day. Hw will choose to attempt to find some kind of video game contents from computer tool which has the attractive entertainment content , it can let he to feel enjoy to play and it is free download from mobile or computer. Then, he won't choose to spend unpredictive time to visit any video game shops to make purchase decision on that day. So, time pressure will be one factor to influence some video game software consumers to feel whether they ought either visit any video game shops to make purchase choice or download some free video game contents at homes for the feeling no enought learning time student players. Even time pressure will also influence adult working people video game players, when the working person feels tries after his full day busy working on that day. Then, he will want to stay at home to rest . Although, he expects to visit any video game shops to choose which video game software product(s) to buy on that day, but when he discovered taht there are some video game contents which ar attractive to influence him to do free download behavior from internet at home. Also, he feels very tried and he will choose to stay at home on that day. If he can find some free video game contents are attractve to influence he chooses to do free download video game contents behavior and replace visiting video game stores behavior on that day. So, free download video game content entertainment activity will be one attractive promotin video game software method to assist the video game sellers' new video game products to let many feeling time pressure learning or working video game players to know from internet channel.

Consequently, online free entertainment video game content download playing choice will influence many video game shops will lose many feeling time pressure video game players number every day in possible. Also, it means that the lazy students or disliking learning students or no job people or (less working hours) part time working people, they will be the main target video game customers, due to they accept to spend much time to visit their video game shops to choose any kinds of video game softwares to buy in preference.

● How can video game advertisement method influence feeling time pressure and feeling without time pressure video game software consumer purchase purchase?

In fact, video game sellers can choose new media chnnel to advestise their new video game software products, e.g. computer online advertisemen channel, instead of video game pictures in shops, magazine, newspapers, television, radio ,cinema, public transportation tools poster traditional advertisement channels. However, computer online advertisement channel can attract many feeling learning time pressure of students consumers and feeling lack of enough rest time working people consumers to let them to choose to view their video game software advertisements from online websites at homes conveniently.

It is easy to understand , due to these feeling lack of enough learning time student video game players and feeling lack enough rest time working people video game players, they go back home after they finished learning in schools or they finished jobs in workplaces on that video game purchase planning day. After they eat their dinners, they may turn on computers to search information from internet. Suddenly, they discover some attractive video game contents photos or images are advertised from the video game seller's website or public yahoo websie , even they can choose to buy any one of these video game softwares from online shopping channel. Then, they will feel convenient to buy any one of these video game softwares from internet channel. SO, online video game advertisement will be the feeling time pressure video game players' first time contact channel at homes or the fastest advertisement contact channel to compare visiting video game store post advertisement, television , radio , magazine contact advertisement channels, when they are staying at homes.

Due to internet is popular to be used to search any information for consumers. So, the traditional magazine, newspapers, television, radio and visiting video game stores advertisement channels won't be more attractive to the feeling time pressure video game consumers . They will chooce to find any information from internet at homes in preference , when they have at least one computer to use at home, they can click website to search any information from internet easily.

The most important factor is that they can feel to spend little time to search information from internet to compare spending more time to find anywhere places whether they has magazines or book stores to sell video game magazine and newspapers publishers, radios and television won't inform them when they have video game advertisements to let they know whether what new video game softwares will promote to sell as soon as possible when they buy newspapers or turn on radios or televisions at home.

Otherwise, internet will be easy to let the feeling presure video game software consumers to know when whose liking new video content game software(s) will be promoted to sell from internet advertisement easily. Also, the feeling time presure video software consumers can choose to buy their liking video game software (s) from online shopping channel in possible if the video game seller can provide one website to let him/her to pay visa to buy and then it can deliver the video game software(s) to his/ her home immediately or tomorrow or later time when the buyer's home located in overseas or far away from the video game seller's warehouse and their softwares are needed to be delivered by air plane transportation.

So, the feeling time pressure video game players won't need to leave their homes to spend more time to visit any video game stores to make final video game purchase decision any time. Hence, online advertisement and shopping channel will be one good sale promotion method to any feeling time pressure video game players nowadays. It will influence the traditional visiting video game stores' video game consumers' purchase behaviors to change to online purchase behaviors at homes conveniently, because they avoid to waste much time to visit video game stores as well as avoid to waste much time to choose any video game products in different video game stores, when they are staying in different video game stores. Visiting video game purchase behavior will need they spend whole day time to make final purchase choice, even it is possible that they can not make any video game softwares purchase decision after they visit many video game stores on that day.

Otherwise , online game advertisment channel can let them to feel to spend little time to search any new video game contents from every web page as well as every web page can show the new video game content images or photos or pictures to let every online users to see clearly when he/she sits down to turn on computer to search any kinds of video game content information to view at home in short time.

In conclusion, online video game advertisement and online shopping channel can attract many feeling time pressure video game players' consideration when they need to search any kinds of new or old video game contents information and it also changes their purchase decision to online shopping from traditonal visiting video game store shopping behavior. Video game industry's advertisement method , sale method is the kind of video game playing content's easy or difficult feeling degree , spending how much playing time to win the competiton in the game entertainment environment factors will influence the feeling time pressure video game players' final purchase decision making choice behavior to any video game software publishers nowadays.

CHAPTER TWELVE

Time queue pressure brings theme park entertainment industry visitors negative emotion

For theme park entertainment industry, when visitors enter to any entertainment theme park , they need to queue to wait long time to play any entertainment machine facilities, which will bring their negative emotions and it can influence they feel not choose to go to the entertainment theme park to play any entertainment machine facilites again. Then, it will be possible to reduce the entertainment theme park visitors number because they can choose another entertainment theme park to replace it. I shall indicate Walt Disney entertainment theme park case example to explain how it avoids visitors feel long time queue pressure to influence their positive entertainment emotion during they are staying in Disney.

In the past Disney background history, Disney had encountered human resource and strategic management etc. different challenges about ten years. How to design its entertainment facilities to attract many visitors to visit and let they feel no any queue time pressure when they have interest to play any entertainment facilities, due to global entertainment theme park competitors are increasing, how to change its image to let visitors to feel it has much different image to compete its competitors. I shall explain how and why Disney needs to arrange entertainment facilities management to avoid any visitors feel time pressure when they need to queue to play as below:

First, what is a tourist destination and space tourist destination difference? e.g. space trip routes, Disney trip routes. Because any Disney visitors can not play all entertainment facilities and visit any entertainment destination in one day as well as any space travellers can not catch the space ship to fly all routes in space in one day. Hence, any Disney entertainment theme park and space tourism companies need provide any suitable space tourism destinations or Disney entertainment facilities destinations to let consumers to choose to entertain.

A tourism destination has many different characteristics. It is one product but also many,

involves many stakeholders with differing objectives and requirements, is both a physical entity and a socio-cultural one, is a mental concept for potential tourists, is subject to the influence of current events, natural disasters, terrorism, health scares etc.is subject to historical, real and fictitious events,

is evaluated subjectively in respect of its value-for-money (based on reality compared with expectations), and differs in size, physical attractions, infrastructure, benefits offered to visitors and degree of dependence on tourism ? In fact no two tourism destinations can be treated the same. Disney ought to choose space travel feactures to attract many visitors, so it ought no choose general earth tourism features because space tourism features are more attractive and fresh ideas to attract visitors, e.g. space toursim related entertainment facilities, space tourism 3 D to 5 D movies to provide visitors to watch to feel who are sitting in space flying boats to travel during they are staying Disney theme park any time. So, they will feel Disney theme park is one space tourism boat similarly.

Second, what are between space tourism impacts and Disney entertainment impacts difference ? Tourism has a far wider range of direct and indirect impacts than other economic sectors. At its simplest tourism can be seen to be a temporary addition to the population of a given location, with tourists having all the needs and impacts that the permanent population does, plus a few more besides. Government planning, regulation etc. is therefore needed; yet tourism is an economic sector executed by the private sector. Tourism activity involves direct contact with the local population. Tourism, then, involves a triumvirate of destination interests ?state, private sector and community.

As such, Disney must let visitors to feel that it can provide space tourism service to let they to play in short time , it is not general tourism servic to satisfy their space toursim entertinment theme park difference. Space tourism planning for development and marketing is unlike any other economic sector and requires special approaches, procedures and institutions. Thus, Disney needs to know that space tourism features are different to general earth tourism as well as what factors will influence whose consumers do not choose to find their entertainment service. e.g. expensive air ticket, too cold or too hot weather, expensive space ship tickets or Disney admission fee , crowd in Disney or space ship etc. different factors to influence whose customers' choices.

Third, what is the difference between general earth tourism and space travel tourism perception? ?what is reality? How between space and earth tourism difference between a destination, or commercial tourism organisation, promotes its products and/or services is a key factor in the realisation of developmental or economic/financial objectives. In an activity like earth tourism where the customer is so far to live from the place he/she is considering to visit. Otherwise, on space tourism perception and reality hand, such as spending long time to catch plan to arrive Disney or space ship destination or what entertainment service he/she is thinking to buy, such as Disney entertainment facilities or space ships facilities. Disney space entertainment tourism marketing is a central component of tourism. Two of the adages of tourism marketing arising from this situation are that:

(1) Disney cannot test drive a earth holiday only? and it ought let its visitors to feel space tourism hoilday in short time enjoyable entertainment feel, such as they can feel that they are sitting rockets to fly to moon to travel in short time.

(2) On Disney short time space tourism, the perception is the reality to its visitors' space tourism feeling in short time?

Disney long time wait queue pressure problem

Wiig, k.(1993) indicated that The Walt Disney Company is one of the largest media and entertainment corporation in the world. Founded on Oct. 16, 1923 by brothers Walt and Roy Disney as a small animation studio. Today, it is one of the largest Hollywood Studios and also owns eleven theme parks, two water parks and several television networks, including the American broadcasting company. Disney entertainment theme park expansion has in recent years focused heavily on Asia, and specifically China, Hong Kong, Japan.

What factors caused Walt Disney strategic and human resource problems ?

In the beginning, Disney underestimated and neglected some strategic and organizational behavior issues which can influence its different departments' operations inefficiently. What factors caused Walt Disney human resource and hotel operational problems?

On the human resource problem hand, Bahandin, G et al., (2009) indicated that" errors are made regarding overall operation for Euro Disneyland from its American experience that Disney throughout Monday would be the light day for guests and Friday would be a heavy day to allocate staffs. In fact to this day, it had not enough staff to supply to staffing at a theme park, where the number of visitors per day in the high season can be 10 times the number in the low season ; wrong operational assumption of bus driver, it built the French bus parking space much too small. Bus drivers were unhappy as they had a very difficult time fitting their buses into their designated spots. In addition, Disney provided only 50 restroom facilities for bus drivers and on peak days there would be 2000 drivers ; operational errors are made to computer involved stations at the hotels. It assumed guests would stay at the park for morning spent the day at the park checked into the hotel late that night, and then checked out early the next morning before heading back to the park. Since there were so many guests checking in and checking out, additional computer station had to be installed at the hotels in order to decrease the amount of time the guests stood in line and hotel counter service staff numbers would also need to be increased. "

On the hotel operation problem hand, Dickson et al.,(2005) also indicated that" it had wrong belief that it understood European breakfast taste and Disney was told Europeans didn't eat sit down breakfast. This resulted in Disney downsizing their restaurants before Euro Disneyland opened. In fact, they were trying serve 2500 breakfasts in a 350 seat restaurant at some of the hotels. Further guests wanted bacon and eggs rather than just coffee. Disney reacted quickly with pre-packaged breakfast delivered to rooms and satellite. Thus, it caused result in Disney downsizing their restaurants."

The reasons showed that French Disney restaurants are caused to fail , such as lacked French cultural characteristics, but only European social and eating pattern ; the non availability of alcohol proved, employees were not expected to be spoken in French language and who also were not fluent in English. Hence, Disney restaurants can not accept French eating style and culture to attract many French visitors to go to Disney restaurants to eat.

Due to, USA Disney did not follow French people eating taste and speaking cultural, It must cause its French restaurant operation unsuccessfully before.

In addition, Disney has wrong judgement to operate its business in USA and overseas Disney operation wrongly. Such as Disney estimated the demand of employee numbers wrongly. It only employed an additional 200 experienced Disney managers were located in the other three centres. In addition, some 4000 employees were unable to find suitable positions. It caused management lacks optimistic assumptions to know who ought to be provided training to its staffing to dealt cultural difference challenges. Moreover, it also had external threats and internal weakness challenges. It included high bank investment interest rates charge , unreasonable working conditions, poor communication and lack of cultural awareness because managers and it caused staff turnover increasing finally. The most failure, before Disney had not carrying on research whether whose visitors feel happy and satisfactory to enjoy its entertainment facilities when who are staying in Disney. Otherwise, who feel unsatisfactory and unhappy , even who need to complaint whose service quality. Hence, Disney numbers of visitors was decreasing before. Such as, visitors felt unhappy because who need to spent much time to queue. It also caused Disney visitor numbers was declining. Thus, Disney will need to consider how to change human resource activities to adapt clients' needs, such as reducing bad emotion to cause visitors who needed to spend much time to queue to wait to play entertainment facilities.

Disney traditional knowledge management strategy

Disney had attempted this traditional knowledge management strategy to solve its human resource and daily business operation challenges successfully. As Harriet Griffey (2010) stated that "sometimes, boredom can give disadvantages to reduce staffs' ability to motive to work and reduces positive emotion , such as happiness. Thus, it causes people (staffs) lack motivated reasoning to unconsciously evaluate evidence in ways consistent with whose preferences. This type of bias can hinder a company's ability to learn from mistakes and to build successful strategies."

However, Disney chose to implement knowledge management strategy to satisfy visitors demands and needs to let who feel more satisfactory when who entered Disney to play its any entertainment as below:

For first example, Disney demanded cleaners to repeat to remember any information to prepare to answer visitors' enquiries. It will train every cleaner memory to remember any information to be long term from short term memory successfully and every cleaner won't feel bore to do only cleaning job duty. When every one feel places are clean, who will concentrate on answering any visitors enquiries as the same time. Even, if they can give excellent service performance to serve visitors to let who to know how to go to any places in the short time. It is possible that visitors will appreciate whose service performance to let their manager to know, so that every cleaner will have chance to raise salary.

Besides for second example, waiting time and queues are daily problem for Disney theme park. Fast lines or priority queues appear as a solution of efficient queues for clients. Disney understood fast ticket line system affected visitor attendance numbers. Disney entertainment facilities long waits leaded to lower service evaluations and greater customer dissatisfaction. Efficient queue waiting time management can improve Disney visitor satisfaction and the willingness to recommend the service. Disney analysed of theme park visitor behaviour in relation to pay the higher ticket price to select to pay more for fast queuing line ticket than common queuing line ticket. In fact, Disney fast queuing line ticket system choice gave potential queues to any waiting clients . In general, Disney visitors don't like to wait long time in every entertainment facilities queuing line, who will feel a waste of time and waiting can lead to negative emotional response like frustration, impotence, tension or irritation .

In fact, Disney amusement theme park needed visitors wait long queues and delays which were a frequent occurrence in every entertainment facilities line. Disney theme park as sets of rides, spectacles and leisure mechanisms are intended to entertainment and spark the imagination of clients, allowing visitors to escape their daily routing. In result, waiting is often a problematic issue that can influence Disney visitor experience and that can appear as one of the principal motives for complaining. As Disney visitor demand fluctuates constantly and demand patterns are often difficult to predict. It caused extra staff needed for the extra line. Finally, priority services such as fast line system facilities segmentation of its amusement park. When Disney offer the possibility of purchases a fast line, which are creating two different group. Disney visitors who are highly sensitive to waiting times are willing to pay to avoid or reduce lines or visitors that are highly sensitive to price that prefer to wait rather than to pay extra money.

Also, Disney provides extensive training opportunity for participants through its own Disney university. The question of whether their training opportunity can lead the improve human resource activities. On the third hand problem, Disney are also worried that employees may leave it and join other competitor to serve their parks after training. Disney shows a trend of increasing depending on human capital other than physical capital. It thinks human capital is the knowledge, skills, ideas and commitment of its employees. It explains that investing in training and development is essential to its client service growth. In fact, Disney had owned enough entertainment facilities, restaurants, hotels, shopping centres within theme park, but its visitor numbers are increasing to need to be served satisfactorily. However, it needs to train cleaners, entertainment facilities service staffs, queuing service staffs, hotels, restaurants, shopping centres service staffs, instead of it's entertainment facilities attraction.

For the final example, Disney observes that spending on training and development is typically regarded as consumption, instead of investment. On job training usually can't be replaced by formal education, therefore Disney chooses to make contribution on providing further training and development to employees. Disney paid salary for staff training, which included classroom, seminars, symposia or conferences; computer based training, on site training, book and periodicals reading, formal mentoring and informal mentoring program opportunities to meet its old staffs and new staffs both needs of motivate factors to achieve advancement , achievement, personal growth responsibility and achievement and recognition to raise its business performance effectively and efficiently.

However, Disney's amount of training has a positive influence on intrinsic motivation of its employees. Job satisfaction, salary, working condition, its policies, administration, relationship with supervisors, peers and subordinates are Disney factors to influence it's human resource activities performance. Disney training contents include these functional area: Raising excellent service performance include that hotel food and beverage service delivery, shopping center, merchandise sale, restaurant service, entertainment facilities queuing waiting service, cleaning and enquiring how to go different locations in Disney, cashier service etc. They are very important to influence visitor numbers. Disney implementation of knowledge management solution to improve queuing waiting line process. The use of Disney front line service staffs as human capital combined with knowledge of customer preference has made the fast pass an innovation solution to enhance queuing in the Disney theme parks. Disney ability to capture customers in virtual queues when giving them a pleasurable waiting experience has made them a leader in knowledge management initiatives in the service industry. Disney's emphasis on human capital within their theme parks, combined with traditional queuing theory to create more pleasurable waiting environments. Hence, Disney showed the value of tacit employee knowledge integrated with traditional queuing theory to reduce loss of customer satisfaction to enhance, goodwill and profitability. Knowledge management expresses itself as human action in form of evaluation, attitudes, points of view, commitments, motivation etc. It seemed that Disney agreed that human capital (people, knowledge, ideas, creativity) maybe today's most valuable commodity.

How to apply knowledge management strategy to solve Disney long time queue waiting playing challenges? Knowledge Management Strategy was used to queue control from Disney. Disney managers have long understand the pressure of waiting time and revenue; who know that every minutes spent waiting in queuing is a minute that the client is not generating revenue. So, Disney managers have processed with design of a reservation system recognizes that guests can be freed from physically standing in the actually and perception of waiting by allowing guests to engage has arrived. Cope et al., (2008) showed that" the system was first tested at Disney in 1998. Managers assessed the system by surveying guests who used it. Results were positive and indicated that guests spent substantially less time in queuing, spent more per capita, and saw significantly more attractions, satisfaction level sky rocketed.The system was expanded in 1999 to include five of the most popular park attractions and was named FASTPASS. The system has since been expanded to all Disney theme parks worldwide, and is now in use by over 50 million guests per year .That guests have two options .Namely, they can choose to Obtain a FASTPASS ticket and come back a later, designed time or Wait in a traditional queuing. Guests are assisted in making their choice by information regarding estimated waits of both options. Thus, can decide to wait in the traditional queuing, or take a FASTPASS ticket and return it a later time with no further wait. Once an assigned FASTPASS time is generated and provided to a guest, it is valid for the 60 minutes beyond that time, creating a window in which guest can return."

There are numerous benefits in allowing park guests to return to an attraction within a designed time frame. Queue Waits involve managing two major client issues:

1.How long Disney visitors actually wait every time queue.

2.How long Disney visitor think they are waiting by whose psychological feeling every time queue.

Thus, if they feel that who spend much time to queue, it will cause they feel angry and they also feel admission ticket price is paid too high to them unfairly. In general, clients were allowed the ability to see two attractions during the time they would have previously been able to see only one. This can viewed as an implementation of a multi-phased system, depending on the attraction picked, each queuing may be single channel attractions, the guest creates whose own multi phase system. Obvious, results, were that guests were able to engage in more revenue producing activities, saw more of the popular attractions and began to par take care, in other less utilized attractions .

Wiig defined(1993)" Knowledge management in different ways and from different perspective. The emphasis is on human know how and how it brings value to an organization. Intangible asset contributes to corporation objective may be immeasurable and isn't simple to evaluate the impacts of knowledge management."

However, Knowledge management may not be only factor influencing organizational performance. In fact, Disney refined technology utilization to improve the user design of all human resource related systems, improving timeliness (queue waiting time deduction), setting elapsed time goals and monitor performance towards those standards, considering to use of automated fast queue waiting system, evaluating staffing levels, a close examination of adequacy of current staff level is warranted, beyond to improve visitors satisfaction. Clients holding fast pass tickets may choose to visit a gift shop or any park concessions. Thus, Disney has ability to co-branded products and service.

Disney's approach combining queuing and human capital. Dunn, J et al., (2002) showed "The use of fast pass provides an insightful application of the combination of techniques of queuing and human capital to strategically leverage knowledge management principle .When waiting lines are an part of the Disney experience, park guests build magical memories through innovation. It is Disney's recognition of front line service staffs that transforms that employees into knowledge who multi task in their roles. For example, an attraction host or a street sweeper may be a valuable Source knowledge to park guests. In addition to their primary roles, they may have a wealth of information about attractions for guests. They may be able to give directions, provide schedules, and offer helpful suggestions from their daily observation. This is the first stop to increase knowledge management . Next, Disney improves its clients' perception by minimizing the perception of waits. The use of the fast pass enables Disney not only to enhance the psychological aspect of waiting lines, but also to capitalize at the same time." Instead, Disney needed to give people specific tools designed to help them to do their job and solve specific business problems. Thus, after Disney learned how it applied the knowledge management method to solve its challenges, e.g. Human capital and queuing theory provide two very different valuable assets to raise its competitive ability. Then, its visitor numbers was increasing largely and quickly.

In conclusion, Disney need to change it's strategy to adapt any the business environmental situation change in different time. For example, in the past, due to Disney had encountered operation challenge and human resource management challenge. So, it apply fast queue knowledge management strategy to solve visitors' spending long queue time is needed to wait to play any Disney entertainment facilities to let them feel satisfactory and feel no angry to compaint Disney. It seems that it is more successful to attract many visitors prefer to pay admission fee to visit Disney to play.

However, nowaday, Disney is encountering another kind of challenge, such as how to let visitors feel that they can spend long time to enjoy any long time and expensive similar entertainment feeling, such as sitting rockets to fly to moon travel feeling. I shall recommend that it can apply space tourism strategy to design its entertainment facilities are similar to space tourism entertainment facilities to let its visitors feel that they can spend short time to sit rockets to travel to moon.

Disney space tourism, is the perception the reality to its visitors' short time flying to moon travel feeling?

Why will Disney entertainment theme park space tourism entertainment facilities attract many visitors?

In fact, space tourism and Disney theme park both businesses which have similar characteristics. Such as they are entertainment business, Disney provides different kind of entertainment facilities to let visitors to play to feel exciting satisfaction as well as space tourism provides one space ship to let travellers spend less time to sit in the space ship to fly to space to see any space stars and let them to feel exciting in the black space environment. They have these similar aspects:

They need have high technological machine facilities to supply, e.g. Disney needs different kinds of machine entertainment facilities to let visitors to sit down to play, Space tourism needs space ships to supply to travellers to sit down to fly to space. They needs to provide high quality of entertainment service to satisfy consumer individual need, e.g. Disney needs often to change its entertainment facilities to let visitors can play any different kinds of new entertainment machines more satisfactory. Otherwise, space tourism needs often to change new design of space ships to let travellers to sit as well as chooses different space trip routes to let travellers to see different space sightseeing when their space ships enter to any different space trip route every time. Due to Disney and space tourism have these kind of similar entertainment factors to cause their business can be success or failure. Thus, I believe Disney knowledge management strategy is similar to space tourism business. I shall indicate these knowledge management strategies which can be applied to space tourism business as below:

When discussing the advancement of space science and space technology, most people think about deep space flights, lunar stations, and thrilling outer space adventures. The fact is that the majority of the human technology in space, which consists of interconnected satellites, points towards Earth, and is used to provide services for and fulfil the goals of people on planet Earth. Over the next decade, there will be an increased need for innovative Earth information systems to support the international space community's efforts to provide a robust infrastructure.

However, space exploration requires vast sums of money. Is the amount of money spent on space research justifiable? Could the money be cheaper spent to let every space travellers? Thus, space tourism will have the effective knowledge management strategy to let every space traveller to feel every space trip fee is very reasonable to satisfy their space trip needs. The space trip service includes many different kinds of space good tasty foods supplies, comfortable and good design and safe environment of space ship facilities, exciting different space trip route choices, the reasonable space trip time length, space flight timetable arrangement, space ship service attendant attitude and performance and space tourism professional technical knowledge. Thus, space tourism business needs have these unique space knowledge management knowledge: Such as space tourism service attendant staff individual space ship service knowledge and space ships safe flight and trip space science tourism knowledge, space foods manufacturing knowledge, space ships repair and crisis management knowledge. If any space tourism company expected whose space travelers have confidence to choose to sit their space ships to go to space to travel safely. Otherwise, even although if the space tourism ticket fee is cheap in common , global space travelers won't prefer to choose to catch any space ships to go to space to travel if who felt any space ships were unsafe and dangerous transportation machine to let they lack confidence to sit safely. Thus, space tourism operators need to consider how to apply knowledge management strategy to let space travelers feel more safe and satisfactory needs more than Disney visitor.

Disney short time entertainment enjoyable feeling
strategy

Disney and space tourism entertainment businesses can consider how marketing policy and strategy might be incorporated in a destination overall Disney space tourism theme park development approach, Disney needs to consider those basic characteristics of space tourism that have implications for the marketing function.

● Fragmentation of space tourism supply

The space tourist product is a composite one, a combination of attractions, transport, accommodation, entertainment and other services. In most countries, there are many separate suppliers of these various components ? Disney theme park needs to supply these unique space toursim characteristics to feel visitors to feel, such as Disney own airlines to be supplied to overseas visitors to fly to Disney by cheap airline ticket fees, Disney supplies space unique characteristics hotels which can let visitors to live in space , space tour excursion organisers supply to let visitors feel Disney is one space entertainment theme park to provide space facilities entertainment services etc.

It is an important feature of Disney space tourism concept that, though an Disney individual supplier of different Disney space entertainment tourist services may serve unique similar space entertainement facilities and space entertainment service than other similar entertainment theme park competitors market, rarely, if ever, does a single space entertainment supplier provide the entire range of Disney space similar products /space similar services required by a tourist on a visit to any destinations in space theme park. Whether sold as a Disney space entertainment cheap package or assembled by the tourist himself or by a Disney space travel agent to give cheaper Disney admission fee price to compare to other travel agent Disney ticker prices , the Disney space tourist product is in practice a composite one. It is apparent, then, that given the fragmented nature of supply on one hand, and the demand for a combined set of Disney space tourism products on the other, a fundamental challenge for a destination is to achieve coordination and integration of all components across all sub-sectors of the Disney theme park entertainment tourism industry - that is, of only one supply to Disney space tourism entertainment theme park only. So, global theme park visitors only feel only Disney theme park can provide unique space toursim feeling when they choose to enter Disney theme park. It means that other global theme entertainment theme park can not provide space tourism experiences to attract them to visit.

● Interdependence and complementarity of Disney space tourism tourist services

It follows from the fact that Disney space entertainment theme park tourism demand is for a composite product that the various general earth tourist products and services are interdependent and complementary. Disney needs to supply the unique space tourism experience to let theme park visitors to feel. The supply of one (for example Disney space tourism theme park international air transport to/from a destination) depends on the supply of another (such as hotel accommodation) and they complement each other. I means that Disney can build one airport which can let visitors to feel it has space travel feeling during they arrive the Disney country.

A Disney space tourism theme park destination reputation can be set by the weakest link in the tourist product chain. This leads to the marketing policies and actions of one enterprise directly influencing other enterprises. A country with a liberal charter policy and/or an airline with an aggressive pricing policy may result in the attraction of low budget tourists, something that could damage the high quality image central to the marketing of a five-star hotel chain in the Disney destination. There is again then the need for coordination and cooperation in order to enhance the effectiveness of individual marketing and promotional efforts of the various tourism suppliers. Due to Disney can have any space tourism airports in every country to let visitors to feel that it is only Disney visitors have qualification to enter to Disney space tourism airports only. So, any non visiting Disney theme park visitors won't have chance to enter Disney space tourism airports when they fly to the owned Disney theme park countries.

In consequence of the intangibility of Disney and space entertainment businesses are tourist entertainment service products, when a supplier of a tourist services considers the potential market, the essential thought process should be: expectations ?experiences ?memories. This is the same whether the supplier is a destination promotion authority seeking to attract tourists to a specific country or location within that country, or the operator of a fixed-site facility like a hotel, restaurant or attraction, or a provider of tour excursion.

Each Disney tourist is a set of expectations. The Disney space tourism product cannot be test driven or known about with certainty in advance of being consumed. The Disney space entertainment tourist therefore builds mental images of the destination and of the facilities and other components of the tourism product of that destination. He/she has a set of expectations about the place to be visited.

Disney space tourism experiences is because the intangibility of tourism products means that the tourist engages in a series of activities ?typically, for example, riding on Disney transport is supplied between airport and Disney theme park, Disney space entertainment facilities visiting attractions, staying in some form of space tourism accommodation, eating, drinking, recreating, interacting with other people ?none of which produce a final physical product to take home. Each Disney space tourism tourist trip, therefore, is a combination of various experiences.

At then end of the trip the tourist is left with nothing more than memories ?the derivation of the word souvenirs - and proxies of the trip ?such as supplying Disney space tourism photos or videos to let visitors who can remember when they visit to Disney to play to feel space tourism experience.

The key for the Disney space tourism marketer is that the expectations created achieve the fine balance between attracting the Disney space tourist while not promising more than can be delivered. The Disney space tourism entertainment experiences are assessed by the tourist against his/her pre-trip expectations. A major determinant of success is how well the experiences match or exceed these expectations. This assessment has relative as well absolute dimensions. A destination may have a perception in the marketplace of being expensive or offering poor service, something which will limit its drawing power. If the Disney tourist finds it is not so costly or that service is better than expected, his/her level of satisfaction will be higher. Of course, the reverse can also be the case with more damaging consequences for the destination.

The intangibility of the Disney theme park tourist product and the consequent need for the marketer to address the potential market perceptions of the tourist product has two dimensions: first, the need to offer unique space tourism psychological benefits to the prospective Disney tourist; and, second, to recognise that the perception is the space tourism reality - with each Disney tourist having sovereign power over his/her destination decision making ?and that Disney space product sale marketing activities should be designed to alter the market prevailing images in line with the marketer desired position.

Disney short time knowledge management strategy

●

●

●

● As Harriet Griffey (2010) stated that "sometimes, boredom can give disadvantages to reduce staffs' ability to motive to work and reduces positive emotion , such as happiness. Thus, it causes people (staffs) lack motivated reasoning to unconsciously evaluate evidence in ways consistent with whose preferences. This type of bias can hinder a company's ability to learn from mistakes and to build successful strategies." However, Disney needed to implement knowledge management strategy to satisfy visitors demand after who entered .Disney demanded cleaners to repeat to remember any information to prepare to answer visitors' enquiries. It will train every cleaner memory to remember any information to be long term from short term memory successfully and every cleaner won't feel bore to do only cleaning job duty. When every one feel places are clean, who will concentrate on answering any visitors enquiries as the same time. Even, if they can give excellent service performance to serve visitors to let who to know how to go to any places in the short time. It is possible that visitors will appreciate whose service performance to let their manager to know, so that every cleaner will have chance to raise salary. Besides, waiting time and queues are daily problem for Disney theme park. Fast lines or priority queues appear as a solution of efficient queues for clients. Disney understood fast ticket line system affected visitor attendance numbers.

Disney entertainment facilities long waits leaded to lower service evaluations and greater customer dissatisfaction. Efficient queue waiting time management can improve Disney visitor satisfaction and the willingness to recommend the service. Disney analysed of theme park visitor behaviour in relation to pay the higher ticket price to select to pay more for fast queuing line ticket than common queuing line ticket. In fact, Disney fast queuing line ticket system choice gave potential queues to any waiting clients . In general, Disney visitors don't like to wait long time in every entertainment facilities queuing line, who will feel a waste of time and waiting can lead to negative emotional response like frustration, impotence, tension or irritation .In fact, Disney amusement theme park needed visitors wait long queues and delays which were a frequent occurrence in every entertainment facilities line. Disney theme park as sets of rides, spectacles and leisure mechanisms are intended to entertainment and spark the imagination of clients, allowing visitors to escape their daily routing. In result, waiting is often a problematic issue that can influence Disney visitor experience and that can appear as one of the principal motives for complaining. As Disney visitor demand fluctuates constantly and demand patterns are often difficult to predict. It caused extra staff needed for the extra line. Finally, priority services such as fast line system facilities segmentation of its amusement park. When Disney offer the possibility of purchases a fast line, which are creating two different group. Disney visitors who are highly sensitive to waiting times are willing to pay to avoid or reduce lines or visitors that are highly sensitive to price that prefer to wait rather than to pay extra money. Also, Disney provides extensive training opportunity for participants through its own Disney university. The question of whether their training opportunity can lead the improve human resource activities. On the third hand problem, Disney are also worried that employees may leave it and join other competitor to serve their parks after training. Disney shows a trend of increasing depending on human capital other than physical capital. It thinks human capital is the knowledge, skills, ideas and commitment of its employees. It explains that investing in training and development is essential to its client service growth. In fact, Disney had owned enough entertainment facilities, restaurants, hotels, shopping centres within theme park, but its visitor numbers are increasing to need to be served satisfactorily. However, it needs to train cleaners, entertainment facilities service staffs, queuing service staffs, hotels, restaurants, shopping centres service staffs, instead of it's entertainment facilities attraction.

●

● Disney observes that spending on training and development is typically regarded as consumption, instead of investment. On job training usually can't be replaced by formal education, therefore Disney chooses to make contribution on providing further training and development to employees. Disney paid salary for staff training, which included classroom, seminars, symposia or conferences; computer based training, on site training, book and periodicals reading, formal mentoring and informal mentoring program opportunities to meet its old staffs and new staffs both needs of motivate factors to achieve advancement , achievement, personal growth responsibility and achievement and recognition to raise its business performance effectively and efficiently. However, Disney's amount of training has a positive influence on intrinsic motivation of its employees. Job satisfaction, salary, working condition, its policies, administration, relationship with supervisors, peers and subordinates are Disney factors to influence it's human resource activities performance. Disney training contents include these functional area: Raising excellent service performance include that hotel food and beverage service delivery, shopping center, merchandise sale, restaurant service, entertainment facilities queuing waiting service, cleaning and enquiring how to go different locations in Disney, cashier service etc. They are very important to influence visitor numbers. Disney implementation of knowledge management solution to improve queuing waiting line process. The use of Disney front line service staffs as human capital combined with knowledge of customer preference has made the fast pass an innovation solution to enhance queuing in the Disney theme parks. Disney ability to capture customers in virtual queues when giving them a pleasurable waiting experience has made them a leader in knowledge management initiatives in the service industry. Disney's emphasis on human capital within their theme parks, combined with traditional queuing theory to create more pleasurable waiting environments. Hence, Disney showed the value of tacit employee knowledge integrated with traditional queuing theory to reduce loss of customer satisfaction to enhance, goodwill and profitability. Knowledge management expresses itself as human action in form of evaluation, attitudes, points of view, commitments, motivation etc. It seemed that Disney agreed that human capital (people, knowledge, ideas, creativity) maybe today's most valuable commodity.

Bibliography

Ansoff, H.I. (1987) Corporate Strategy. Penguin, London

Bahandin, G. & Guerganna, K.S. United States, (Jan. 2009).Strategic human resource management and global expansion lessons from the Euro Disney challenges in France. International business & economics research journal, vol. 8, no.1.

Barnard, Bruce: Business is booming in the world's biggest tourist market, March 1999, p.22, Journal of Commerce, Brucells.

Barnard, Bruce: Business is booming in the world's biggest tourist market, March 1999a, p.24, Journal of Commerce, Brucells.

Benesch, Dieter, 1989: " Theme parks in Florida-Eine Analyse von Angebot und Nachfrage sowie Regionalwirtschaftliche Auswirkungen" , Master 's Thesis at the University of Economics and Business Administration, Vienna. AAdvisor: Prof. Dr. Karl Sinnhuber, Library.

Brennan, L. & Vecchi, A., (2011). The Business Of Space, The Next Frontier Of International Competition. Palgrave Macmillan Press: USA, New York.

Charles B. (2012) Curiosity Takes Us Back to Mars the WHITE HOUSE Available at: Date Of Publication: 6 Aug. https://www.whitehouse.gov/blog/2012/08/06/curiosity-takes-us-back-mars

Cope, R. R. Cope and H. Davis (2008). Disney's virtual Queues: A strategic opportunity to co-brand services ? Journal of Business & economics research, vol. 6 no10, 13-20.

Dickson, D., R. Ford and B. Laval (2005). Managing real and virtual waits in hospitality and service organizations. Corncell hotel and restaurant administration quarterly, vol. 45 no1, 52-68.

Dunn, J & A Neumsister (2002). Knowledge management in the Information age. E. business review, Fall , 37-45. Jounral of service, spring 2011, vol. 4, no1, De Grovte (2009).

Edinger Tourismberatung GmbH: Study: "Die Entwickling von Freizeitparks in Osterreich, 1998, for: Bundeministerium fur wirtschaftliche Angelegenheiten, wien" Innsbruck.

ERA (Economics Research Associates) 1998: " The Future Role of Theme parks in International Tourism" , Clive B. Jones & John Robinett, Los

Angeles, p.5

ERA (Economics Research Associates) 1998a: " The Future Role of Theme parks in International Tourism" , Clive B. Jones & John Robinett, Los Angeles, p.13

Foden, harry G. 1996, " Destination attractions as an economic development generator", Economic Development Review, Fall 1996, 10., American Economic Development council

Friedmann, David:" Status Report of the Los Angeles County Economy", Vol.1, prepared for the "Los Angeles Board of Commerce, 1999.p.78

Futron Corporation (2009) Resource Centre. Available at:http://www.futron.com/resource_centre/resource_cemtre.htm.

Gartrell, R.B. (1994) Destination Marketing for Convention and Marketing Bureaus. Kendall/Hunt Publishing, Dubuque, Iowa

Harriet Griffey. (2010) The art of concentration, enhance focus, Reduce, stress and achieve move. Macmillan publishers ltd,Basinastoke and Oxford, London UK.

Hertzfeld, H.R. (2007) Globalization, Commercial Space And Space Power In the USA, Space Policy, Vol.32, no 4. November.

IAAPA: International Accociation of Amusement Parks and Attractions (http://www.iaapa.prg), " Theme Park Industry at-a-a glance" (Brochure), 1999, Atlanta, Georgia.

Kotler, P., Bowen, J. and Makens, J (2003) Marketing for Hospitality and Tourism. Prentice Hall ?Pearson Education, New Jersey

Kotler. P., Hamlin, M.A., Rein, I. and Haider, D.H (2002) Marketing Asian Places: attracting investment, industry, and tourism to cities, states & nations. John Wiley & Sons (Asia) Pte. Ltd., Singapore

Kotler, P., Haider, D.H. and Rein, I (1993) Place Marketing. Free Press, New York

Kyriazi, Gary, "Amusement Parks: A Pictorial History" Secaucus, NJ: Castle Booka, 1997.

Lundberg, Donals E. (ph.D.): " The Tourist Business", 1995, 5. Edition- Published by Van Nostrand Reinhold Company, New York.

Middleton, V.T.C. & Clarke, J. (2001) Marketing in Travel & Tourism. Butterworth Heinemann, Oxford

PKF consulting, 1997: " Study of the Projected Future Tax for: The City of Anadheim, the Anaheim Public Financing Authority, Nov. 13, Collections From Designated Sources to be Received by the city of Anaheim", 1997, prepared -1997.

Tarasenko, M.V. (1996) Evolution Of The Soviet Space Industry, Acta Astronautica, Vol. 38, no. 4-8, pp. 667-73.

The Economist 1997: "The Los Angeles economy: Bigger than South Korea", Feb, 4. 1997 page 25-26, London.

Wiig, k.(1993). Knowledge management foundations: Thinking About thinking. How people and organizations create, represent and use knowledge vol.1 , of knowledge management series schema press: Arlington, TX.

Yip, GS. (2003) Total Global Strategy II: Updated For The Internet And Service Era (Upper Saddle River, NT: Presentice-Hall).